GODDESSES

OF HIGH MAGIK

DAVID THOMPSON

GODDESSES

OF HIGH MAGIK

FOUR POWERFUL GODDESSES TO HELP RESHAPE YOUR LIFE

HIGH MAGIK BOOK 8

DAVID THOMPSON

Goddesses of High Magik

ISBN: 9781961765061
PB Edition
TransMundane Publishing

A Legal Disclaimer:

By Law, I am obliged to let you know that this is for entertainment purposes only, and does not claim to prevent or cure any diseases. The advice in this book should not be construed as financial, medical, or psychological advice. Please seek such advice from a professional.

By purchasing this book, and working the rituals, you understand that results are not guaranteed. In light of this and in the unlikely event that this course does not work for you or, in the very unlikely event, this book causes physical harm to you or a loved one, you agree that you will not hold David Thompson, our affiliates and employees liable for any damages you may experience or incur.

Each individual's success depends on his or her background, dedication, desire, and motivation.

A Warning:

This material has the ability to profoundly influence people and make a significant impact. If the work is done properly, you may observe outcomes that you did not anticipate. Just like how electricity flows in the direction of its intended output, the energy generated from performing these rituals and petitions will also flow towards the desired outcome. In saying this, please be firm in your intentions and make absolutely sure what you want is truly want you desire.

As they say, be careful what you wish for, you just might get it.

To Fortuna, Goddess of Wealth and Fortune
To Lilith, Goddess of Power and Fame

"Science is always discovering odd scraps of magical wisdom and making a tremendous fuss about its cleverness."

— Aleister Crowley

PART ONE

INTRODUCTION

Magik has been present since the dawn of human consciousness. It was a common practice for tribes to have a magician, whether a man or a woman, who would use magic to ensure good hunting, prosperity, and the overall well-being of the tribe. Those were known as shaman or medicine man/woman and were tribal magicians with a profound bond to the spirit world.

In the era preceding the rise of monotheistic religions, a significant shift occurred in the spiritual beliefs and practices of humanity. During this transformative period, the prevalent concept of an omnipotent sky father emerged, gradually supplanting the earlier reverence for the earth mother.

However, it is of utmost importance to acknowledge that prior to this transition, goddesses played an essential role in the lives of individuals and communities alike, assuming diverse forms and embodying various aspects of existence. The realm of magik was well-known for its practice of incorporating and summoning powerful goddesses. It was quite common in many tribes and social groups for goddesses to be the ruling deity, which is a testament to the vital role that these divine feminine figures had in shaping and guiding society. Their influence resonated deeply, infusing both the collective and personal realms of human experience with their grace, wisdom, and nurturing qualities.

The vibrant tapestry of magikal practices during this time honored the interconnectedness of the earth, cosmos, and humanity, weaving a rich spiritual heritage interwoven with goddesses' profound presence.

And to those deities, I dedicate this book.

Lately, my magik book writing has centered around the goddesses of magik, particularly Lilith and Astaroth, who demanded that I write about them. Other goddesses who wanted their stories to be told saw an opening with this. Multiple goddesses have appeared to me in meditation and dreams. Their persistence is evident as they request to be included in a book or have a book dedicated solely to them.

I have worked with both gods and goddesses (daemon or otherwise) and I prefer the energy of most goddesses. It's softer energy, except for Lilith in her daemonic form. The results are just as quick as with a god/daemon.

In this book, I'll examine a small selection of underused elder goddesses, all of whom are eager for their presence (and power) to be known. I will illustrate a female aspect of an established daemon, which symbolizes powers and talents not completely acknowledged by the male aspect.

This book results from the cooperation of all four goddesses who shared their stories with me and allowed me to write them in their own words. Occasionally, like with the goddess Haurvatat, I experienced images, sounds, and emotional energy that made me feel like I was experiencing their first journey into this world.

We start with Gremory, a daemon found in the lesser seals of Solomon.

Next is Skadi, a little-known Norse goddess

Then Marchosias, mis-identified as a male entity for several hundred years

Then I look at an ancient deity from Persia, the Zoroastrian goddess of health and wealth, Haurvatat. Early tests of rituals to Haurvatat were impressive. I wish I'd known about her a year ago, then maybe I'd have avoided a life-threatening event a few months ago. She's an elusive spirit, and not a lot is known about her except for a handful of references in Zoroastrian writings.

I'll not only go over their history, as given to me by the spirit, I'll cover their preferred methods of contact, along with some very powerful sigils. These sigils can be turned into permanent medallions or altarpieces, or simply printed out and activated.

After I cover each of the goddesses, I'll present some magik sequences for wealth and money, and some magik sequences for love (One always needs a section on Love magik when talking about goddesses. It's their number one talent.).

The times of day, days of the week, and moon cycles need not be taken into account when working this magic. The effectiveness of this magik is not dependent on the timing of the rituals; it will work no matter when they are performed.

In addition, I will be presenting my own form of pathworking for each spirit during which I will also include their respective daemonic form, if one exists.

One thing to note, before I move on: Gods have been here both forever and just today.

Seriously.

If you have moved over from a brand name religion to the magik tradition(s), the established god you once knew is just ONE of a multitude of gods. Or Daemons, who're actually out of favor gods, so it's just a label. To you, suddenly, these ancient gods are new to you. Though, they've been around almost forever.

And by forever, I mean as far as humans have recorded histories. Which is quite limited, honestly. Like a thin, crusty layer of ice on top of several feet of snow.

In my channeling and research while writing my first magik book, Hermes, he gave me a historical timeline for *HIS GROUP* of gods/goddesses.

But there are as many differing pantheons as there were tribes in ancient times.

Like Hermes, some gods moved from one pantheon to another. Not as complete as the shift from Greek to Roman, where the Romans simply dusted off the Grecian gods and gave them new names (and not even that with Apollo).

Many gods can be connected back to the destruction of a previous civilization, one not hindered by human's concepts of religion (which hinders a society's spiritual growth). In these societies, meditation, spiritual growth, recycling of lives, and the use of mental powers like magik were quite common. As one grew, they eventually became what Hermes termed "Immortal Masters", meaning their physical bodies shifted into a higher dimension and they literally turned into god-like beings.

Then the comet came. Those masters stayed on, to assist the survivors in rebuilding. Hermes, as Thoth, help create what we call Atlantis. Then these masters stayed, assisting the survivors of Atlantis in creating our current civilization timeline.

During the more tribal portions of this timeline, early humans began to create egregores. An egregore is an energy being that is created by the thoughts and actions of the human mind, usually a group. At this point, the more interesting gods emerged. Gods with antlers, Goddesses who were worshiped by entire groups of people, focused energies who became gods worshiped by multiple tribes, as word of their powers spread. Some, like Lilith, evolved over time to be quite powerful goddesses.

Thus, from our limited points of view (some people are more limited than others) these gods have been on earth forever.

What are the origins of Odin? I'm looking into this. He appears to be a variation of the Zeus/Jupiter energy. The same holds for the entire Norse Pantheon.

Similar to the Celtic Pantheon, where the goddess Eostre feels similar to the energy of Aphrodite/Venus.

In this book, I have done the hardest selection process I have ever done, selecting only four Goddesses from the thousands of goddesses in history. Three that I have recently discovered, one I have worked with for a while, and two popular goddesses.

What do they all have in common?

These goddesses are also Goddesses of Wealth!

Gremory, Skadi, Marchosias, and Haurvatat!

CHAPTER ONE

Manifesting via magik - The basic process.

Is it Manifestation? Or is it "magik?"

It's just a matter of terminology. People often refer to it as manifesting in the New Age community, but the truth is that it is just another form of magik. Magik is a practice that involves using various techniques to manipulate and harness the energies that surround us in order to manifest our desires into reality. In contrast to what we see in movies, books, or television shows, magik is not capable of bringing things into existence out of nowhere or making things disappear.

If you really want something to disappear, tell the universe you need to hide the object where you can later find it, and it'll disappear for good. Trust me, this works all the time.

Magik has no limitations except those that you put on it. It takes the same amount of focus and intent to manifest a hundred dollars as it does to manifest a million dollars. So, which do you think, right now, you can manifest? I can manifest hundreds of dollars by intent and focus alone. Add in an ancient, powerful goddess, and I can manifest a few thousand.

So, how does that work? When you read the rituals on the following pages, you will notice a few important phrases being used in the petition and spoken out aloud. "Shift time and space" or "Alter my history". These are important requests of the goddess. We can use them in any petition, not just the ones in the following chapters.

One thing that works against any magik is inertia, where the situation will tend to stay in its current state (you being poor or being single) until a sufficient outside force is applied, plus we must also deal with entropy, or the randomness of our universe.

One thing that works for us in magik is the concept of multiple worlds. Along with this are multiple potential time-lines.

By asking the divine being to "shift time and space", you are asking them to place you in a time-line where the desire manifests. By going backwards, the events that will shape your new future will have already occurred.

Taking action.

Often, to make magik work, one will need to perform some physical action. I've gone over this in previous books, so I won't repeat myself here. However, it does no good to manifest a monumental shift in your life if you're not willing to "let go" of the past, or do the physical work needed to help the magik.

The other task for you is to determine what it is you really wish to manifest.

Once you've done that, then you need to simplify how you ask for it. The more complex the request, the longer it takes the magik to manifest. Especially if you place a lot of restrictions on the magik. For example, if you need a few hundred dollars, try not to place a deadline or a method of delivery on it. Say things like "Bune, please see to it I receive six hundred dollars as fast as possible."

Bune is known as THE money demon. I'll pathwork and ask for an increase in my bank balance, and he will deliver.

The Petition

As in my other books, you will need some type of written petition to present to the divine being after you summon them, unless you simply wish to obtain answers to questions or have them hang out with you for tea and cookies. (Don't laugh: plenty of magicians will do this.)

I typically make my petitions short enough to fit easily on a small piece of 5 (in) by 3 (in) paper. Any paper will work, but the smaller the better, as you will be advised to burn the petition during the ritual and a large sheet of paper might make a bit of extra smoke. (Note: This is optional. Some people say you must burn the petition, others say you keep the petition. In my tests, it didn't make a bit of difference, so each to their own.)

I will use a fountain pen to write the petition. I will fill the pen with a small amount of prepared "magic" ink, which is plain fountain pen ink with a drop of my blood. (Note: This does NOT take the place of a proper blood offering during a ritual to a Goetic being.) You may use whatever you have around you, just make the pen and ink "special". Use the pen only for petitions, or use a feather quill pen and some ink. Any ink will work, but use only fountain pen ink in a fountain pen, or it'll likely clog later. I always clean my pen I use for petitions after a ritual, placing the unused ink back into the bottle.

What do you desire?

No really, what is it you want?

Deep side. Dig deep. Often, what we desire isn't what

we actually need.

Without putting in some effort, we can't easily find what we need.

For example, you feel you need a new car. This may be because your current car is always breaking down. Pretty straight forward at first glance. But what you really want to manifest is *reliable transportation.* Okay, you can run a ritual to one goddess, and ask for reliable transportation that you can afford, and receive the desire as fast as possible. This might manifest as a good used car a neighbor is selling, or you find an inexpensive mechanic who knows your current car and can make it reliable for very little money.

Conversely, you can petition Haurvatat for the money for a new car. My advice is to make a careful request to Haurvatat for the money for a new car, including the phrase "money arrives safely, and no one is harmed" in the petition.

In 1994, I did a ritual for a new car. I visualized a modern style, in green. A month later, I was at a dealership and the same model car was available, at my price point, in maroon. Did I pass and ask for a green car? No, I quickly traded in my old truck for this lease return, and that car lasted me 12 good years. I had it 14 years, because those last two years were tough.

My petition was simple, a new car. My visualizing did more to lock in the type of car and the plain petition.

Visualizing

This is the key to all magik: fully visualizing the outcome.

As a writer, I'm pretty good at visualizing a scene and getting that down on paper. I also use visualizing to plan a photograph. By fully visualizing the scene, it helps me in planning and executing a book or a photograph.

The distinction between visualizing and manifesting and simply daydreaming is quite subtle. If visualization is a major part of magic, why can't daydreaming also bring about a manifestation? The answer lies in the concept of intent and the directed force of your will. Daydreaming without a specific intent is simply daydreaming. However, add deliberate intent, combined with force of will and you can perform magic.

Prior to working these rituals, you might want to consider practicing visualizing. Since you are not in ritual, practicing visualizing is an excellent way of preparing for your ritual. While writing your desire down, try visualizing the outcome. Look at all the various ways the desire might manifest. Then move past the *HOW*, to just focusing on the desire manifesting, simply showing up in your life. Step back, and look for any loopholes, or issues your desire manifesting might cause, and make adjustments.

When doing the visualizing for the new car, I didn't go into details, just the general shape of the mid-1990s car, plus a color. Then I added "highly reliable and long lasting" … and then I let that thought go.

While accompanying a model to a dealership to get a car, I saw the car that I would later purchase, even though I had forgotten about the ritual I had done. I wasn't intending to buy anything, but that car was just there and waiting.

I drove that car for a decade and a half before selling it. This is what I mean by "highly reliable and long lasting."

Detaching from the Outcome

That is the hardest aspect to magik, ever. So, this is what I've previously written on this subject:

Let go of expectations regarding the outcome. It is crucial to approach manifestation with a sense of detached curiosity. Open yourself up to receiving. This involves creating room in your life for the object of your desire. Be grateful for what you already have. The more gratitude you feel, the more abundance you will attract into your life.

On my Facebook group, I ask members to post their successes and what they're thankful for on a weekly basis. You can post in my group, or simply keep a journal of your successes. By giving thanks and listing successes, you can see how your power grows as you learn and practice magik.

Ritual Preparations

When preparing a ritual to one of these goddesses, at the very least you will need her sigil, your petition, and some type of offering. These are elder goddesses, and, as such, they are expecting offerings more in line with what they used to receive in their temples in ancient times. Fruit, such as dates and raisins. Grain or bread. Fresh flowers and sometimes perfume or incense resins. Perhaps the most desired offering would be frankincense resins, since this was a highly prized and much sought after in those times.

When working a full ritual, decide on which items you will need. I prefer to work with fewer items on my altar than most. A candle, incense, offering, and the petition usually works for me.

Items needed:

Altar candles
Goddess sigil
Dedicated goddess candle
Offering and Offering bowl
Incense and incense burner
Petition and fireproof bowl

To this list, you may add other items such as crystals

and special altar cloth, oils to enhance the magik, such as "Crown of Success Oil", etc.

Each goddess has a set of preparations unique to her own magik, which you will see in the following sections.

Preparing Your Petition

In most cases, a ritual will need a petition. The exception is that after working with a goddess or demoness for a long period, you might be able to dispense with a formal petition.

In the older books I've read, the petition or spell was to be written out on "virgin parchment". True parchment was an animal skin that could be reused by cleaning the ink off the surface. In this way, true parchment was highly valuable and asking you to use "virgin parchment" indicated a way of sacrificing in order to work the magik.

It is my experience that we only need nice paper. Not a discount stationary pad found at a discount store, but something nice, with thicker paper, such as 120gsm note paper.

In each ritual that follows, I will give you an example of a petition for that goddess or demoness. I urge you to use that as a template, and not copy it word for word. This way, you can customize most any ritual to fit a specific situation.

Write in regular ink, but you can also use "magik ink".

I've never purchased this ink. I have always made my own. It's a simple formula, where you can take any fountain pen ink, using an eyedropper to put a small amount of ink into a tiny jar, then use a sterile diabetic lancet to poke a finger and put a drop or two into the jar, and mix. I use a cheap fountain pen to write my petitions, and then sign it. You can use plain ink or pencil for your petitions, no need to hunt for magik ink. Remember, all magik depends on your intention, not any one specific ritual item.

Sanctifying your space

Each ritual will instruct you to purify your space at the very beginning. Unless you keep a dedicated room to your altar, expect some stray energy/spirits to be in your space. You can eject these energies in one of two ways: Smudging the area with incense like frankincense, or using a pendulum to clear the energy in the area.

Smudging:

Please don't expect sage of any type to purify a space. While it's common to hear about using sage to smudge negative energy, it's important to remember that its original use by Native Americans was to help them get into the right head-space for performing their rituals. Their energy always purifies their space. It's an energy barrier they send out that prevents any unwelcome spirits from being in their lodge.

I will smudge my space using pure frankincense resin in a censor, allowing the smoke to really flow through the space. Be careful not to trigger any smoke detectors in your space. The sudden loud alarms can ruin the focus needed to sanctify your space.

You really don't need to say or chant any special words, unless you feel it'll help your situation. I just assume I've ejected the unwelcome spirits, and that assumption works as an effective energy barrier.

Pendulum:

This is a more physical method to clear the energy. You are still using your own energy to clear the space, but using a pendulum allows you to focus a bit more clearly, which causes the cleansing and sanctifying result.

Start at one wall, or edge, of your space. Hold the pendulum in one hand and relax. Ask the pendulum to swing as you clear the space. The pendulum will begin to swing, usually in a circle.

As it swings, tell it to send out clearing energy. The harder it swings, the stronger the energy.

Walk around your space, allow the pendulum to continue swinging, and as you walk around, the pendulum should begin to slow down, as the unwelcome energy is dissipated.

Typically, the process takes just a few minutes and eventually, the pendulum will gradually come to a stop.

There is no requirement to speak, just the intention of clearing your space will be enough.

Modifying a Ritual

The rituals in this book are generic, meaning that you can use them for any desire with only changing the ritual candle. With Gremory and Marchosias, you need to decide which aspect to use, as the daemonic aspect handles different tasks. The daemonic aspect's rituals are designed around the traditional daemonic rituals, as seen in many grimoires. While they are both generally pleasant, it's still advisable to monitor their actions closely.

You can also simplify most of the rituals once you are used to working with each goddess. The basic items needed will be a candle, sigil, offering and petition, everything else is optional.

Failing magik

Yes, magik can fail.

In fact, at first, most magik practitioners will see only

a 20-30% success rate.

If you perform a ritual wrong, for example, the magik will not backfire or cause problems, it'll simply not work.

Failing magik has nothing to do with working the magik wrong, it usually is because what you are trying to manifest might not be actually possible. For example, attracting a specific person as a lover is usually the most difficult magik outside of trying to levitate or fly. It CAN work, and has worked for me and others, but it's a 10 out of 10 difficulty rating.

Success at magik will increase as you work magik. As you continue to use magik and experience its effectiveness, your confidence in its power will grow, resulting in a higher success rate. In fact, the success rate can exceed 95%, which means that the possibility of failure is negligible.

Like driving a car or flying an airplane, your confidence increases the more you practice it.

PART TWO

THE GODDESSES

Ancient Goddesses

The goddesses I'll be looking at in this book are all from a group of deities I call "Elder Gods". You might want to call them "The Old Ones", or Ancient Masters, or any other name, but they originate in antiquity. They predate modern civilization by several millennia.

Tribes from all corners of the world have worshiped these gods. The major gods evolved from these gods, growing in strength, until the present day.

Unlike the modern gods, the elder gods do not demand fealty. The occasional offering of wine, bread, or other easily found item. Some may ask for a blood sacrifice, such as uncooked meat, or a drop of your blood. Devoting yourself to the goddess through prayer for consecutive days is not necessary, neither is devoting yourself to her, unless you feel a strong connection and decide to make her your main goddess and set up an altar in her honor.

It's not a requirement, it's purely voluntary.

Many of these elder gods are now called “demons”. Or, more accurately, “Daemons”. The difference? Daemons are helper spirits, given the collective name of “Daemon” during the Greek classic era. In my mind, “demon” is reserved for those really dark beings, truly negative energy, capable of harming humans, usually by scaring them. Humans, when scared, are capable of some serious self-harm.

How do you know if a spirit is a “Daemon” or a “Demon”? For myself, I get a good feel of the energy and I get flu-like symptoms. I feel as if I have a fever, my ears get plugged, and I feel dizzy. If I have summoned a powerful, but truly dark spirit, this is how I know it has arrived. I try not to summon these, but sometimes people need to be taught a lesson that Lilith or another daemon can’t deliver properly.

While it is true that many people have worked or are currently working with these energies, this book’s unique approach is to take you back in time and work with the original energies associated with these goddesses.

And now, through the mists of time, they call to you.

First up, Gremory.

Gremory

Listed in Ars Goetia, as demon number 56, and gives her ranking as a Duke (Duchess). Despite the fact that contemporary practitioners of the occult often consider Gremory to be a female spirit, ancient writers generally perceived all mighty beings as male.

Gremory is known by many names, such as Gemori, Gomory, Gamory, Gaeneron, Grimorio, Momai Maa. 3. The traditional powers that are commonly believed to be possessed by this spirit include the ability to predict the future, uncover hidden treasures, and even help a man win the affection of a woman. Casual readers will immediately see the potential for money magik with Gremory, and the single practitioners will see potential for soft love rituals. Soft, in that Gremory will not drag someone to you (see Lilith) but will encourage the targeted individual to seek the petitioner.

Her demonic ENN is "***An tasa shi Gremory on ca,***" and is traditionally spoken three times while summoning her. Often, the ritual includes commanding an angel, Shemhamphorasch angel Poiel, although this is actually needed unless working one of the more Abrahamic styled rituals calling upon all the protective angels, then on Gremory. That's up to you, but this book will not list that as one of the rituals for her, and instead I'll present a way to work her as a goddess, with goddess results.

As a goddess, some of the expected issues with Gremory the Daemon do not manifest. She does not try to trick you, will not act wicked and cunning like some daemons, and operates in a way that is in the highest good of the petitioner.

The process of performing the ritual to Gremory as a daemon is not complicated, however, it is crucial to be accurate while petitioning her in this aspect, as she is known to grant what you ask for, but it may not be what you truly desire.

Origins

Gremory seems to have simply appeared, about mid-century in the 1500s, with the writing of the Pseudomonarchia Daemonum. But direct contact via channeling reveals a fascinating history:

Her original energy leads me to maps of early Eastern Europe, which is now called Ukraine. I am pulled to the earliest tribes of humans, long before the later city-states evolved. It feels like this could be a pre-Cimmerian culture inhabiting that region around 1700 B.C.E. She was a general family deity, often called upon in times of difficult childbirth. Many of our current daemons originated in this area, which were derived from several hundred minor deities. Sorath is one such daemon, including early forms of Astaroth and Lilith.

She is reputed to have been raised by Paimon, but this places her a lot later in history than the story she gave me. However, there isn't a lot written about her until we get to the daemonic texts of the 15th and 16th centuries. She is reputed to have been one of the daemons summoned and enslaved by Solomon, which placed her into the various grimoires of the late Middle Ages.

She is also seen as the same essential energy as the Hindu goddesses, Durga and Momai Maa. By comparing her to these two deities, we can get a sense of what can be accomplished when using Gremory to manifest desires.

Although the origins of Gremory remain unknown, this divine being has proven to be remarkably advantageous whenever summoned utilizing the techniques that were revealed to me during an extensive series of channeling sessions that lasted for several days.

Goddess Gremory

The process of summoning and collaborating with Gremory as a goddess can result in an immense release of energy that can be utilized to bring about the fulfillment of a desire.

When working with Gremory, you can either

approach her in her daemonic aspect, or use a completely different approach, which brings her in her goddess form. A lot like Lilith and other mislabeled goddesses.

Although a standard demonic ritual has been included and many people summon her in this aspect, my intention is to delve into the goddess aspect of this intriguing spirit and I would like to explore this with you.

Her goddess energy appears just as strong as her daemon energy, but is more suitable for manifesting desires like attracting lovers/soulmates. When it comes to magik, there are times in the business world where you may need to use it to nudge someone gently in a specific direction or to align circumstances in your favor. This is especially true when starting your own business.

Her daemonic energy is best used for manifesting desires that depend on manipulation of others, such as influencing a boss to give you a raise, a potential employer to offer you that awesome job, make someone come to you who was previously resisting.

In either aspect, you can leverage her magik to bring to you wealth and success. Even though using her goddess form may take more time during the ritual, Gremory's magik will be accomplished with minimal fuss and no risk of collateral damage, such as being involved in an accident to obtain a large sum of money through suing an insurance company or the other driver.

Offerings

As is custom with any ritual to a deity, an offering is given when finishing up the ritual. Gremory appreciates flowers, donuts, rolls, wine, and spirits. Place the offering on her Goddess sigil. Have it sit at least overnight, then discard the offering. If possible, pour any liquids outside onto the ground, and any sweet breads leave out for the birds. With flowers, place in some shrubbery or in compost.

Don't offer her your blood, as this is only for her daemonic form.

Goddess Ritual to Gremory

This goddess ritual is pretty straightforward. Since you are dealing with a goddess form, elaborate precautions shouldn't be necessary (see Chapter One on preparations), some protection might be needed, depending on your situation. As I keep a permanent altar space, I only have to purify once in a while, versus when I used my bedroom which was frequently intruded by the other occupants of the house for various reasons.

Items needed:

Altar candles

Goddess sigil

Dedicated goddess candle, Silver or White

Offering and Offering bowl

Incense and incense burner

Petition and fireproof bowl

Begin by lighting the candles and making sure you have everything you need on your altar.

Lights go off.

Next, casting the traditional circle and getting rid of any outside negative energies hanging around your space. You can start by fumigating the area with incense. Then face each direction and trace out your circle. (See appendix on circle casting in a Goddess Ritual)

Once this is done, face your altar and look at Gremory's sigil. Take a deep breath and begin to let go of any tension or stress, allowing yourself to ease into the alpha head-space.

Think about the magik you are about to perform. Visualize at this time the goddess working to assist you in manifesting your desire.

Now, say the following to properly summon Gremory:

Goddess of the celestial sphere, hear me now.

Goddess Gremory, goddess of wealth, family, and health.

Hear me, Goddess Gremory, you who are timeless and eternal,

Grace me with your presence.

Join with me now, here in my space,

Hear me, Goddess Gremory, please listen to my prayers and/or petition:

At this point, read your petition.

Once you have read your petition, take a few moments to visualize again the results of your desire manifesting. Then, (this is optional) you may burn the petition in the fireproof bowl to seal the pact. While the pact paper burns, say:

As this petition is burned, a pact is formed, and it will be executed quickly harming no one.

Now, continue with the offering. Pick up your offering, and say:

Goddess Gremory, to express my deepest gratitude for your working on my behalf, I offer to you this humble (your offering).

Place the offering on her sigil, and it's time to close the ritual.

Before dismissing Gremory, say these lines: **"Gremory, with our combined power, we shall sift time and space, to allow my desire to manifest!"**

You may close this ritual in any way that suits you, or you can simply say:

This ritual is done, and I ask that you leave in peace, and come again when I next call.

Allow the offering to stay on Gremory's Goddess sigil overnight, then dispose of it as I instructed earlier.

Pathworking Gremory the Goddess

This mental only exercise will set your vibrational level to match that of the higher planes of existence, the realm of the gods and goddesses.

As with my previous books that contain pathworking, I am defining pathworking as a simple set of visuals one can work, which places you on the energetic path to communicate with a specific being, be it god/goddess or a daemon.

Start by relaxing and making sure you won't be distracted. Turn off cell phones and televisions. If you are in a public place, perhaps put in some noise-canceling headphones and play some soothing music. Sit and get comfortable.

Then, when you are ready, begin the visualization.

A beautiful garden, flowers blooming. The smell of flowers is in the air.

A path leads past some large, flowering trees.

The sun on your skin.

You see a flock of brilliant blue birds fly overhead.

As you follow their flight, you see a beautiful woman walking towards you.

This is the Goddess Gremory.

Greet her, and ask her to grant your petition.

Read your prepared petition (same as in a ritual)

Wait for her answer

Accept whatever answer she gives. If she declines your petition, ask what you can do to rewrite the petition so she can accept it. Make a note of this answer.

Smile and thank the Goddess for her time and listening to your petition. As soon as you can, make an offering to her using the suggestions in the standard ritual.

Do the following visuals to end the ritual:

You watch as the Goddess departs the same way she arrived.

Turn and walk away.

Open your eyes.

If she accepts your petition, follow up as soon as possible with a simple offering to her.

Place the offering on a printed copy of her goddess sigil.

The ritual is now complete.

Gremory Goddess Sigil

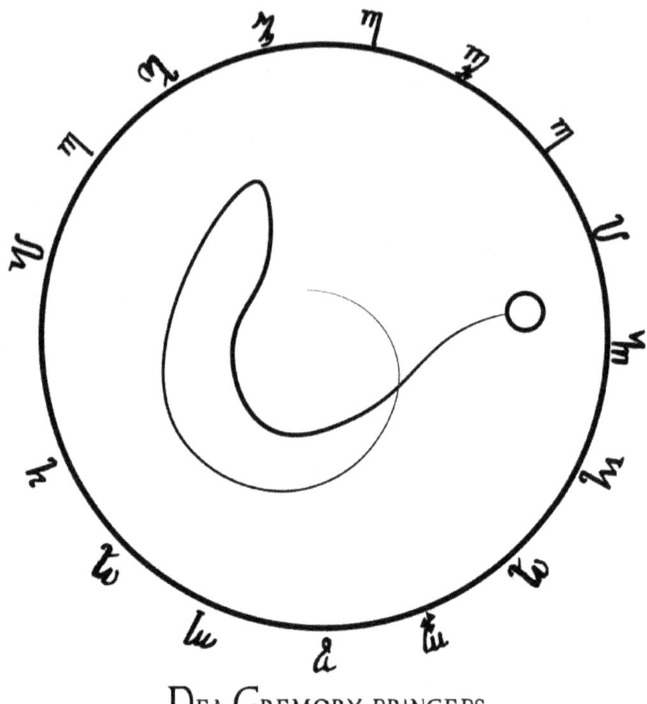

Gremory the Daemoness

As a daemon, the medieval texts depict Gremory as a mighty Duke of Hell, often described as having the appearance of a beautiful woman or a woman with the crown of a duchess. However, Gremory is said to possess the ability to change forms and can manifest in different ways depending on the summoner's desires or needs.

Gremory is said to possess extensive knowledge in various domains, particularly in the realm of secrets, hidden knowledge, and matters related to love and relationships. The demon is believed to have the power to reveal hidden treasures, locate lost items, and provide insight into the past, present, and future. Gremory is also said to be skilled in matters of seduction and can influence people's feelings and affections.

In the old texts, summoning Gremory often requires specific rituals and invocations, typically performed by experienced practitioners of the occult. The demon is believed to be bound by certain rules and can be compelled to answer questions or perform tasks, but caution is advised when dealing with such powerful entities.

Gremory's seal in the Goetia is also a bit hard to draw quickly, so I channeled her and asked for a simplified sigil, which is in this chapter and in the appendix. One method of summoning Gremory is to say a Psalm, then the ENN. Most other methods simply use her ENN. My method uses her ENN, but with a simplified ritual which is still safe and effective.

Colors and Candles

Gremory has many colors associated with her energy.

Red: Red is a common color associated with Gremory, representing passion, power, and the fiery nature of the daemon.

Black: Black symbolizes mystery, secrecy, and the hidden depths of Gremory's powers. It is often associated with the occult and the supernatural.

Purple: Purple represents royalty, wisdom, and spiritual enlightenment. It is also associated with Gremory's ability to provide insights and knowledge.

Blue: Blue is often associated with Gremory's calm and collected demeanor. It signifies tranquility, intellectual pursuits, and the ability to communicate effectively.

Green: Green is connected to Gremory's association with nature, growth, and healing. It symbolizes fertility, abundance, and the restorative aspects of the daemon's powers.

Incense

For this, stick to resin incense if possible. Choose a pure frankincense, followed by sweet myrrh and white copal. You may also mix a blend using those resins. Crush, do not powder the resins and mix in equal amounts.

Offerings

When working the initial ritual to the Daemoness, it is expected to offer a drop of blood as a traditional daemon offering.

Once initial contact has been done, you can ask her what she prefers, or continue to use a single drop of blood. Don't be surprised if she suggests an offering such as red wine.

Daemoness Ritual

In contrast to the Goddess Gremory ritual, here's a brief demonolatry ritual to Gremory, in her daemonic aspect.

Like some goddesses I've written about before, Gremory has two basic aspects. The Goddess and the Daemoness. It's wise to dedicate a specific candle to her for these rituals.

Items needed:

Altar candles
Daemon sigil
Dedicated Daemoness candle, black or white
Offering and Offering bowl
Incense and incense burner
Petition and fireproof bowl

Begin by lighting the candles and making sure you have everything you need on your altar.

Lights go off.

Next, casting the traditional daemon circle and getting rid of any outside negative energies hanging around your space. You can start by fumigating the area with incense. Then face each direction and trace out your circle. (See appendix on circle casting in a Daemon Ritual)

Once this is done, face your altar and look at Gremory's sigil. Close your eyes and let yourself drift into a state of relaxation, entering the alpha head-space. Open your eyes, and trace over Gremory's sigil to activate it.

Think about the magik you are about to perform. Visualize at this time the goddess working to assist you in manifesting your desire.

Now, say the following to properly summon Gremory:

An tasa shi Gremory on ca

An tasa shi Gremory on ca

An tasa shi Gremory on ca

Gremory! Daemoness of power, I ask that you now join with me in my space.

I have a request, Daemoness Gremory!

Now, read your petition aloud.

Pause a moment or two, staying in the Alpha state. Visualize the results of the magik manifesting. Spend some time on this, going into as much detail as possible.

Now say, with as much feeling as you can:

Gremory, I ask that you shift time and space, altering my history to allow this desire to manifest!

Optional: Burn the petition while saying

As this petition is burned, a pact is formed, and it will be executed quickly, harming no one.

Once this has been done, it's time to give over to the Daemoness the offering, using one of the suggested daemonic offerings.

If using a drop of blood, use a diabetic lancet and prick a finger. Place a single drop of blood onto the smaller of one of her sigils, then burn it in the fireproof bowl, while saying:

> **Gremory, in gratitude for your assistance in this magik, I now give over to you this drop of my essence.**

Now, time to dismiss Gremory:

> **Our time together in this circle with Gremory has ended. I ask now that you depart as you came, in peace, and please come again when I next call upon you.**

The ritual is now complete. If you gave an offering that wasn't blood, allow this to sit on her sigil overnight, then dispose of it in nature (if possible).

Pathworking the Daemoness Gremory

This mental only exercise will set your vibrational level to match that of the higher planes of existence, the realm of the gods and goddesses.

As with my previous books that contain pathworking, I am defining pathworking as a simple set of visuals one can work, which places you on the energetic path to communicate with a specific being, be it god/goddess or a daemon.

Start by relaxing and making sure you won't be distracted. Turn off cell phones and televisions. If you are in a public place, perhaps put in some noise-canceling headphones and play some soothing music. Sit and get comfortable.

Then, when you are ready, begin the visualization.

Field of flower in bloom.

Sounds of bees in the flowers.

A path leads into a forest.

Following this path, you now see an opening.

This opening is lit in golden sunlight.

Say Gremory's ENN:

An tasa shi Gremory on ca

You will see Gremory appear to you. She may look like any beautiful woman, greet her with respect, then present your request.

It's optional to write out your petition, but it helps to have it in your hands. That way, briefly open your eyes and read the petition.

Once you've read the petition, look back to Gremory. She'll let you know if she will act on your petition.

Once this is done, thank her for listening to you, using a phrase similar to "Lady Gremory, I thank you for listening to my prayer.

As soon as you can, make an offering to Daemoness Gremory, using the suggestions from the standard ritual.

Gremory Daemonic Sigil (Traditional)

Gremory Custom Daemonic Sigil

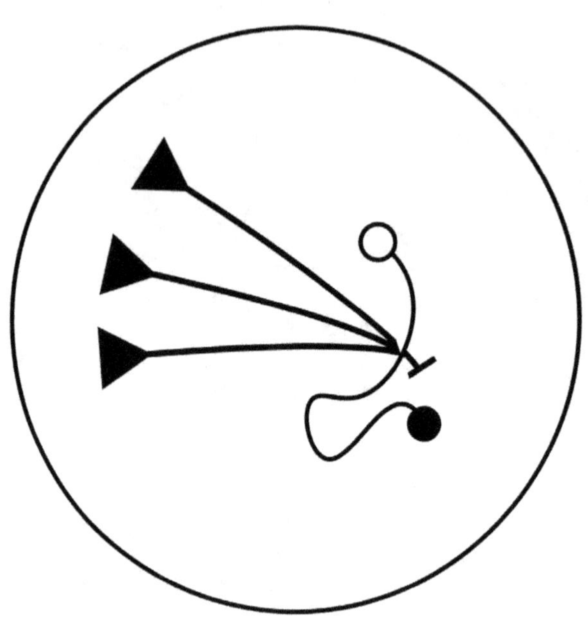

CHAPTER TWO

Skadi

Skadi is a well-known goddess in the Norse pantheon. Pronounced “Ska-Dee”, which rhymes with “Scotty”.

Although she may appear different to you, to me she manifests as a medium height woman with deep red hair.

In Norse myths, Skadi was once married to the god Njord, but the marriage was unsuccessful as Skadi missed the mountains and Njord missed the sea. They eventually separated and Skadi returned to her home in the mountains. Skadi represents the harsh and unforgiving nature of winter, as well as the freedom and wildness of the mountains. She is also a symbol of the power and independence of women in Norse society.

Which makes her perfect for protection magik, as well as any magik involving the family, and little known to outsiders, she is really skilled at uncovering hidden wealth. I worked a brief ritual to her when I started this section; the idea was to figure out what she prefers in a ritual, such as colors and other items she may want in the ritual.

I reached out and made contact, asking her about her origins. I got this in a channeling session:

She originated as a nature goddess in what is now Sweden. I got initial feelings of a cold, snow-laden landscape inhabited soon after the glaciers retreated. She was mostly worshiped and appeased to ensure healthy children and bountiful hunting. They crafted her earliest icons from small bones and animal hides, but then the art shifted to carvings out of antler and larger bones. They did not depict her in the same way earth goddesses were seen, with the heavy breasts and round hips, but more of a huntress in the same mold as Artemis, lean and athletic.

With the changing of society over time, her form has become increasingly defined as that of a huntress and as a guardian of the family and home. In their primitive huts, there were often only small offerings of animal skin and offal left, which were given in the hope that Skadi, the goddess of hunting, would assist the hunters in killing elk or other large animals.

Let's take a brief look at the details of a ritual for Skadi. Information is very scarce regarding this fascinating goddess, so most of this is based upon my researches and in sessions with the goddess herself.

Colors for Skadi

Skadi is often associated with the colors white and silver. She is a goddess of winter, mountains, and hunting, and these colors symbolize the icy landscapes and snow-covered mountains often associated with her realm. Sometimes, Skadi wears furs, which people can associate with shades of brown and gray.

Using these colors will help her spirit feel comfortable in your temple space.

Incense

The aromas associated with Skadi would be those found in forests such as pine and fir trees, incense with earthy and woody notes as well as spices, such as cinnamon and clove.

These incense blends can be found easily enough, but avoid the overly "perfumed" incense common in most shops. I have used Nag Champa (the spicy, Mother's Incense one), along with Morning Star Patchouli and Nepal Juniper incense, which has the aroma of burning cedar bark.

Offerings

She is used to receiving scraps of animal flesh, bones

and fur. She suggested simpler offerings, such as smoked fish bits, wild berries, mead, honey, cream and candies.

I don't have a "daemonic" ritual as Skadi was never demonized, but I offer a simple pathworking.

Skadi Goddess Ritual

Although there is a lack of a vast compilation of prayers and summonings specifically devoted to Skadi in the remaining Norse literature, it is still possible to craft your own personalized prayers and summonings based on her unique attributes and exceptional qualities.

Here's an example of a prayer we can use as a starting point:

> **Great Skadi, Goddess of Winter, With bow in hand and skis upon the snow, I come before you to seek your blessings.**
>
> **Mistress of the frozen lands, Grant me strength and resilience in the coldest of times. Teach me to endure and embrace the trials of winter, As you do with unwavering spirit.**
>
> **Skadi, Lady of the hunt, Bestow upon me your keen senses and precision, That I may navigate life's challenges with grace. Guide my**

arrows true, both in the literal and metaphorical hunt.

Goddess of independence and determination, instill in me the courage to stand tall and face adversity. Help me find my path, unyielding and resolute, As you did when you sought justice for your father.

Skadi, hear my words and accept my humble offering. May your frosty breath invigorate my spirit, and may your blessings carry me through the harshest winters. Hail Skadi, mighty goddess of the frozen north!

Verbose, but useful for initial contact, if you so choose to use this prayer.

For a Skadi ritual, you will need:

Altar candles in white or silver

Goddess sigil

Dedicated goddess candle, Silver or White

Offering and Offering bowl

Incense and incense burner

Petition and fireproof bowl

Since she doesn't pose a threat to anyone summoning

her, we use a simpler circle casting compared to some daemons. Cast a circle using golden light to facilitate the communication between you and the goddess.

Once this is done, face north and calm your mind. A couple of deep breaths, and visualize your desire manifesting with the help of this goddess. Take your time.

Pick up her sigil. Trace the lines with your finger, activating the sigil.

Now, the suggested summoning:

Great Skadi, Goddess of Winter, I come before you to seek your blessings.

Goddess Skadi, I ask that you now join with me and hear my request,

You have comforted thousands of petitioners for thousands of years,

Goddess of the Hunt, Goddess of hidden wealth,

I ask now that you join with me.

Again, pause a few moments, and see if you can detect her arrival. Take another deep breath, and then read your petition.

Pause again, and visualize the results of your petition manifesting. Take as long as you need.

Try now to visualize Skadi near you, dressed in furs,

a hunting bow on her back. She'll be nodding and agreeing to assist you in manifesting your desire.

Once you are satisfied you have visualized enough, say the following:

Goddess, I ask that you alter time and space, shift my reality, and allow this desire to manifest!

Now, give her the offering and say:

Goddess Skadi, in gratitude for listening and acting upon my desire, I offer to you this humble (your offering). Thank you again for being with me!

Now it's time to end the ritual. I usually say something like this:

Goddess, our time together is now at an end. You may depart, go back to your land of mountains and forests, and please come again when I next call upon you.

That's it. The ritual is completed.

Pathworking Skadi

The imagery you will use reflects the areas where Skadi usually lives, mountainous terrain, cooler weather, forests of firs and pines.

This mental only exercise will set your vibrational level to match that of the higher planes of existence, the realm of the gods and goddesses.

As with my previous books that contain pathworking, I am defining pathworking as a simple set of visuals one can work, which places you on the energetic path to communicate with a specific being, be it god/goddess or a daemon.

Start by relaxing and making sure you won't be distracted. Turn off cell phones and televisions. If you are in a public place, perhaps put in some noise-canceling headphones and play some soothing music. Sit and get comfortable.

Then, when you are ready, begin the visualization.

Cool air across your arms and face.
A hiking path through a dark forest.
Look up and see the tall pine trees.
You walk down this path.
In a small clearing is a campfire.
A woman is tending the fire, and looks up
It's Skadi.

Take a moment to greet the goddess, and observe how she appears to you. Chances are, she'll now smile. Greet her and then ask for her assistance. Read your petition, and await her reaction.

If she speaks to you, try to make notes and recall what she says.

To end this pathworking, visualize the following:

Tell the goddess how grateful you are for meeting with you.

Bid her farewell.

Turn and follow the path away from the opening.

See yourself on the side of a mountain.

This concludes the pathworking.

As soon as you can, place an offering on her symbol or sigil.

Skadi Goddess Sigil

Skadi

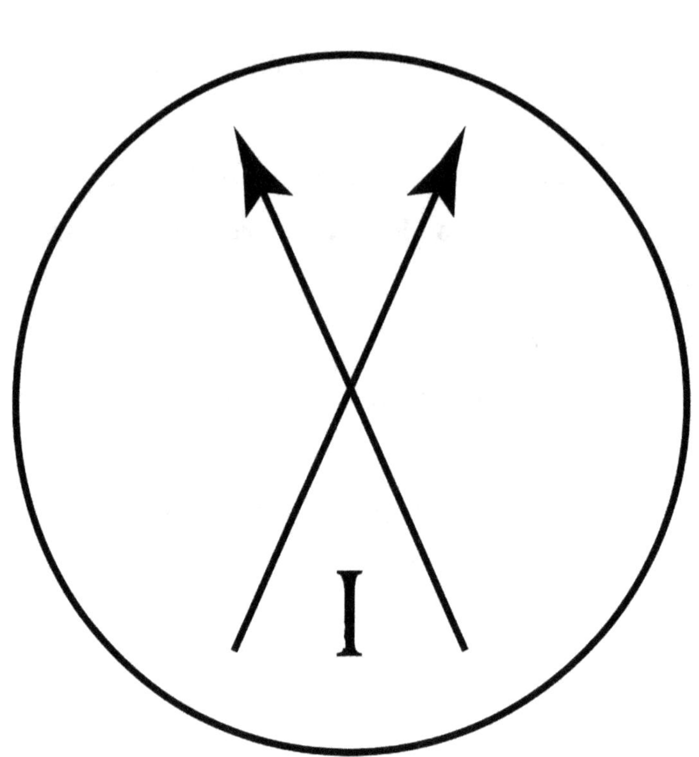

CHAPTER THREE

Marchosias

According to various grimoires and occult texts, Marchosias is described as a powerful demon or spirit who is associated with the infernal hierarchy. Marchosias is often depicted as a mighty marquis of Hell, appearing as a wolf with wings and a serpent's tail. Marchosias is often pronounced **"mar-chosias"**

In the Ars Goetia, which is a book of the Lesser Key of Solomon, Marchosias is listed as the 35th demon. According to the Ars Goetia, he (she) is a great and strong marquis who commands 30 legions of demons. According to the Ars Goetia, those who summon Marchosias can gain insights into hidden things, reveal secrets, and receive protection from their enemies.

But - Marchosias is a feminine spirit and comes to us as a complex egregore.

What can we do with this complex spirit? From my

researches, I have found the following common uses of her in ritual:

Marchosias is a demon who is renowned for her power of divination and discernment, as she is believed to have the capacity to uncover secrets and obscure knowledge. Individuals who call upon her have the opportunity to request her aid in gaining insights, divining the future, or uncovering hidden truths.

Protection: Marchosias is said to have the power to protect those who invoke her from their enemies or from spiritual harm. She is often regarded as a powerful guardian or defender.

Strength and courage: As a mighty marquis, Marchosias is associated with strength and courage. Some practitioners may call upon her to instill bravery, resilience, or physical strength.

Shape-shifting: Marchosias is often depicted as a wolf with wings and a serpent's tail, suggesting an ability to change form or manifest in different ways. This shape-shifting quality may symbolize adaptability and versatility.

Commanding Legions: Marchosias is said to have dominion over 30 legions of demons. This suggests her influence and authority over other infernal entities. Some practitioners may invoke her to gain control over or communicate with other spirits or demons.

By incorporating Marchosias's ENN (*Es Na Ayer Marchosias Secore)* into any daemonic ritual, you can achieve success in invoking her without difficulty. She possesses the ability to handle most any petition as a daemon, but her energy works a bit "rougher", for lack of a better term. Therefore, I still advise you to work the petition so that no one is harmed in the delivery of your desire.

Now, let's collectively toss all that out the window and look at Marchosias as a divine spirit, a goddess.

Goddess of Change

Marchosias, a goddess, has the capability of bringing change either suddenly or gradually, based on the circumstances. Overtime, she is useful in a set of sequential magik, causing this change over the course of the sequence.

The advantages of implementing gradual change over sudden change lie in the fact that the latter could create chaos that was not intended.

Later in this book, I'll present some rituals that use sequential rituals, any of which can be modified for most any circumstance.

We can also work on any issue using her talents as a daemon, just use the goddess ritual in its place. A simple matter of using a different invocation and offering.

Colors and Candles:

Besides colors of candles, you can also use these colors in altar cloths, or other decorations on your altar.

Red is often associated with power, strength, and vitality. It symbolizes energy, courage, and action, which can resonate with Marchosias' role as a powerful and courageous goddess.

Black is often associated with mystery, protection, and the occult. It represents hidden knowledge and the ability to delve into the depths of the unknown. Use black to trigger her powers to reveal mysteries and hidden messages, as well as when asking her questions.

Gold or yellow are colors associated with wisdom, knowledge, and enlightenment. Marchosias' ability to unveil secrets, discover hidden wealth, will be triggered when using these two colors.

Incense:

Frankincense and Dragon's Blood are intimately linked with magik, and would be an ideal choice for summoning the goddess. I'd use 2-parts frankincense to one part Dragon's Blood mix for invoking her as either daemon or goddess.

Here are some other ideas for incense, especially useful for summoning the goddess aspect of Marchosias.

Patchouli: Patchouli is known for its grounding and transformative qualities. It is often used in rituals involving personal power, transformation, and accessing hidden knowledge. The deep, earthy scent of Patchouli can create a conducive environment for working with Marchosias.

Cedarwood: Cedarwood has a purifying and protective quality. It is associated with strength, courage, and spiritual grounding. The woody and grounding aroma of cedarwood can help establish a connection with Marchosias and create a protected space for communication.

Myrrh: Myrrh resin is often used in rituals related to divination, spiritual insight, and connecting with higher realms. It has a sticky and mildly sugary scent that can produce a holy atmosphere for calling upon Marchosias.

Offerings:

As a daemon, she needs the usual blood sacrifice, a single drop of blood on her sigil is sufficient. As a goddess, she communicated to me she prefers offerings of sweet breads and muffins, pastries (especially cinnamon rolls with icing), seasonal flowers in red or yellow, spirits like light wines, and finally she'll be quite happy with an offering of fresh fruit.

As with all offerings, allow these to sit overnight on her sigil, then take them somewhere and dispose of them. With edible items, try to place them outside where animals can find it and enjoy the food.

Marchosias Goddess Ritual

This goddess ritual is pretty straightforward. Since you are dealing with a goddess form, elaborate precautions shouldn't be necessary (see Chapter One on preparations), some protection might be needed, depending on your situation. As I keep a permanent altar space, I only have to purify once in a while, versus when I used my bedroom which was frequently intruded by the other occupants of the house for various reasons.

Items needed:

- Altar candles
- Goddess sigil
- Dedicated goddess candle, gold or yellow
- Offering and Offering bowl
- Incense and incense burner
- Petition and fireproof bowl

Begin by lighting the candles and making sure you have everything you need on your altar.

Lights go off.

Next, casting the traditional circle and getting rid of any outside negative energies hanging around your space. You can start by fumigating the area with incense. Then face each direction and trace out your circle. (See appendix on circle casting in a Goddess Ritual)

Once this is done, face your altar and look at Marchosias's sigil. Take a deep breath and begin to let go of any tension or stress, allowing yourself to ease into the alpha head-space.

Think about the magik you are about to perform. Visualize at this time the goddess working to assist you in manifesting your desire. Trace over the sigil using your finger, or a black ink pen.

Now, say the following to properly summon Marchosias:

Goddess of Change, Goddess Marchosias, hear my call;
Goddess of Divine power and influence;
Goddess of Wealth and Power, Goddess Marchosias;
Speed to me and join with me in my space.
I ask that you alter time and space,
I ask that you shift the past,
And allow my desire to manifest!
Goddess Marchosias, I have a request:

At this point, read your petition.

Once you have read your petition, take a few moments to visualize again the results of your desire manifesting. Then, (this is optional) you may burn the petition in the fireproof bowl to seal the pact. While the pact paper burns, say:

As this petition is burned, a pact is formed, and it will be executed quickly harming no one.

Now, continue with the offering. Pick up your offering, and say:

Goddess Marchosias, to express my deepest gratitude for your working on my behalf, I offer to you this humble (your offering).

Place the offering on her sigil, and it's time to close the ritual.

You may close this ritual in any way that suits you, or you can simply say:

This ritual is done, and I ask that you leave in peace, and come again when I next call.

Allow the offering to stay on Marchosias's Goddess sigil overnight, then dispose of it as I instructed earlier.

Marchosias Daemonic Ritual

This daemonic ritual is pretty straightforward. Since you are dealing with a daemonic form, elaborate precautions might be necessary (see Chapter One on preparations). As I keep a permanent altar space, I only have to purify once in a while, versus when I used my bedroom which was frequently intruded by the other occupants of the house for various reasons.

Items needed:

- Altar candles
- Two of Marchosias' sigils
- Dedicated daemonic candle, gold or yellow
- Diabetic lancet
- Incense and incense burner
- Petition and fireproof bowl

Begin by lighting the candles and making sure you have everything you need on your altar.

Lights go off.

Next, casting the traditional circle and getting rid of any outside negative energies hanging around your space. You can start by fumigating the area with incense. Then face each direction and trace out your circle. (See appendix on circle casting in a Goddess Ritual)

Once this is done, face your altar and look at Marchosias's sigil. Take a deep breath and begin to let go of any tension or stress, allowing yourself to ease into the alpha head-space.

Think about the magik you are about to perform. Visualize at this time the her in her daemonic form working to assist you in manifesting your desire. Trace over the sigil using your finger, or a black ink pen.

Now, say the following to properly summon Marchosias:

Es Na Ayer Marchosias Secore
Es Na Ayer Marchosias Secore
Es Na Ayer Marchosias Secore
Daemon of change, daemon of hidden wealth,
Daemon of protection, daemon of courage,
Speed to me and join with me in my space.
Marchosias, I have a request:

At this point, read your petition.

Once you have read your petition, take a few moments to visualize again the results of your desire manifesting. Then, (this is optional) you may burn the petition in the fireproof bowl to seal the pact. While the pact paper burns, say:

As this petition is burned, a pact is formed, and it will be executed quickly harming no one.

Now, continue with the offering. Prick a finger using the diabetic lancet, place a single drop of blood onto one of her sigils, then touch it to a candle flame, and drop it into the fireproof bowl and allow it to be totally consumed by fire, all while saying:

Marchosias, please accept a drop of my essence as an offering in gratitude for you attending to my petition in a timely manner.

Place the offering on her sigil, and it's time to close the ritual.

You may close this ritual in any way that suits you, or you can simply say:

This ritual is done, and I ask that you leave in peace, and come again when I next call.

The ritual is complete.

Pathworking Goddess Marchosias

Marchosias is a spirit of the underworld, even as a goddess. Thus, this pathworking will involve caverns and darkness.

This mental only exercise will set your vibrational level to match that of the higher planes of existence, the realm of the gods and goddesses.

As with my previous books that contain pathworking, I am defining pathworking as a simple set of visuals one can work, which places you on the energetic path to communicate with a specific being, be it god/goddess or a daemon.

Start by relaxing and making sure you won't be distracted. Turn off cell phones and televisions. If you are in a public place, perhaps put in some noise-canceling headphones and play some soothing music. Sit and get comfortable.

Then, when you are ready, begin the visualization.

You stand at the opening of a small cave,

You walk a well-worn path that leads into the cave.

It's dark, but you can distinctly see the walls of the cave.

The cave hallway opens out into a large

cavernous room

The walls are glowing in pink and blue light

Seated on a rock by an underground stream is the goddess

She looks up and greets you

Take a moment to observe how she presents herself to you. First, please extend a warm greeting to her and then kindly request her assistance. Read your petition. It is important to pause and pay attention to her actions, as well as any verbal cues she may give you.

To conclude this pathworking, visualize the following:

You turn and walk along the path, through an opening, then out into the fresh air.

Follow the path down the side of the mountain.

The ritual is done at this point. As soon as you can, make an offering to Marchosias, with her sigil and suggested offerings.

Marchosias Traditional Sigil

Marchosias Goddess Sigil

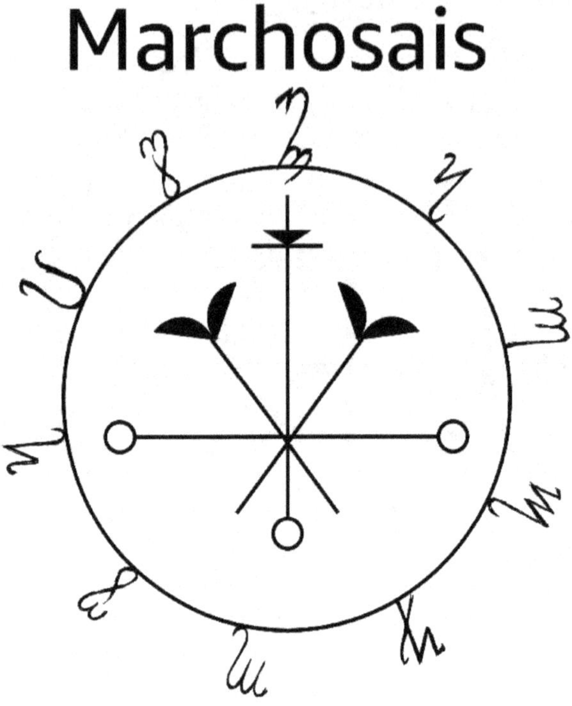

Marchosais

CHAPTER FOUR

Haurvatat

Haurvatat, or "həʊrvətət" is Avestan language word for the Zoroastrian concept of "wholeness" or "perfection." The spirits associated with this word was transformed into one of the divine spirits during the cultural shifts that occurred when Gathic Zoroastrianism declined. Her name means literally water, prosperity and health.

Her preferred pronunciation is **HA-UR-AH-VA-TAT**

To summon her, we will be using some prayers attributed to Zoroastrian texts

To understand this goddess, you need to try to picture what life was like in the middle east, about twenty-four hundred years ago. This goddess appears to have been worshiped and given powers by her followers.

At first glance, it appears Haurvatat is an ancient spirit who inspired the creation of egregores in later generations, but in my contacts with her, I picked up hints of an earlier life. She has been around since the days of Lemuria (or as she put it, Anclatari, which means "homeland" in one of her original languages.)

One of the goals of the early civilizations was to

master the body and spirit, and by doing do, translate into a semi-etheric body. This allowed them to continue to interact and teach the others. Their society was split between those who were devoted to mind/body/spirit and those who began using technology instead of spending their day meditating. At the end, the Lemurians were governed by the spiritually minded people, and when their scientists discovered that an asteroid was on an impact course with the earth, they elected to allow it to occur. The Immortal Masters literally ascended into the astral and then returned to assist in rebuilding.

These Immortal Masters later became what we call gods.

Has Haurvatat always been around? She developed some different aspects when she was worshiped in the millennia after the initial Zoroastrian cultures began to shift towards the newer religions, with the newer gods and goddesses. She maintained her presence as a "Mother-goddess" and in myths was relegated to simply giving birth to the other, more colorful gods and goddesses.

Ritual Preparation

A ritual to Haurvatat is like a ritual to any other spirit. A quiet space for your altar, a few candles, incense, a sigil (or two), and your petition.

Offerings to this goddess need to be kept simple: Sweet breads, high-quality frankincense resin burned as the offering, basic red wine (the libation), a single drop of blood on her sigil.

The biggest part of preparing for this ritual is the petition. Haurvatat is a goddess of wealth and prosperity, but her powers are great (if underutilized) and she can assist in most any manifestation you desire. Being a writer, I can reduce a desire into as few words as possible. And that is what you need to do as well. You also need to work down into all the layers of your desire to find the correct phrase to say in order to manifest exactly what you desire and not what you asked for.

The difference is that what you ask for might not be what you actually desire.

With that in mind, plus my writings on this subject from the other goddesses in this book, I'll now show you how you might want to phrase your petition to Haurvatat. She likes a lot of praise, and is used to the old prayers to her that used to be heard all those millennia ago. If you've read ahead and looked at the ritual itself, you can get an idea of how to phrase a request.

This is just an example, change it to fit your own way of speaking and to fit your needs.

"**Lady Haurvatat, I have called you near to ask for your favor, I ask that you assist me. I wish to win a large sum gambling.**"

Or "**Lady Haurvatat, I ask that you honor me by blessing my business, so that my business now flourishes.**"

Or words to that effect. Haurvatat is a goddess of prosperity and wealth, but she is also very good at love, family, and sex magik. Use her powers carefully.

Types of magik

After several weeks of working with Haurvatat, I have established that she is capable of many modes of magik.

Ritual to Haurvatat

This ritual doesn't need a great deal of props or a complicated altar. A basic candle for the goddess, her sacred symbol, and some traditional incense, like frankincense.

We begin by casting a standard circle and ejecting any negative energies:

Face north, aim a finger, a wand, or a crystal point at a spot on the floor. Imagine light, gold or yellow, flowing from your hand. Slowly, trace out a circle on the floor. This defines the magik circle.

Once this is done, face north again and cast out any negative energies by saying:

Only that which I invite is allowed to remain in this sacred spot. All others must depart now!

Spend a moment or two visualizing the outcome of your desire manifesting. Take your time. With Haurvatat, see her helping make this manifest.

Next, pick up her sigil and trace along its design, activating the image.

Now, we call on Haurvatat:

Ahura Mazda spoke unto the lands, and saying:

"I created for the faithful the help, the enjoyments, the comforts, and the pleasures of

Haurvatat."

I call now for Haurvatat to join with me in this sacred space,

For Ahura Mazda thus commanded the Amesha-Spentas

To follow the commands of his followers, thusly,

And to sacrifice unto Haurvatat that which she enjoys,

Thus, I offer libations!

Thus, I offer my essence

Thus, I bless the sacrifice and prayer, and the strength and vigor of Haurvatat, the mistress

of the prosperity of the seasons and of the years, the mistress of holiness.

Haurvatat - hear my pleas:

Read your petition at this point.

Haurvatat, I thank you for attending to my plea, and I now offer to you this ________.

I ask for your blessings and assistance in manifesting my desire! Please enchant this

(candle/sigil/etc.) to quickly draw to me my desire, and with your help, my desire will arrive swiftly!

Pause again, and visualize your desire/manifestation having already happened.

To close the ritual, say: **Haurvatat, again I thank thee for your presence here. This ritual is now complete and you may depart in peace, and come again when I next call upon you.**

As with the other rituals, leave the offering in place overnight, then dispose of as instructed earlier.

Pathworking Haurvatat

This mental only exercise will set your vibrational level to match that of the higher planes of existence, the realm of the gods and goddesses.

As with my previous books that contain pathworking, I am defining pathworking as a simple set of visuals one can work, which places you on the energetic path to communicate with a specific being, be it god/goddess or a daemon.

Start by relaxing and making sure you won't be distracted. Turn off cell phones and televisions. If you are in a public place, perhaps put in some noise-canceling headphones and play some soothing music. Sit and get comfortable.

Our goal is to connect with the desert goddess Haurvatat, and thus we will be utilizing visuals that depict the arid and rugged terrain of the desert.

Then, when you are ready, begin the visualization.

Hot dry breeze on your face

A sandy landscape, hot sun overhead

See, in the distance, a collection of palm trees

An oasis with green grass surrounding the small pond

Palm trees move in the breeze. It's now cooler.

A woman lounges on the green grass, the breeze blows her veils.

Approach her and sit with her

The goddess is here with you now. Take a moment to greet the goddess, and see how she presents herself to you, what form she has chosen.

Now that she is available, feel free to ask for her assistance and proceed to read your petition.

Pause and visualize the desire manifesting with her help. If she speaks to you, try to make notes and recall what she says.

Now, time to close the ritual. Take a minute to thank the goddess, then visualize:

You turn and walk away from the oasis

The sun hot on your face

Feel excitement over your desire about to manifest.

The pathworking is now complete. As soon as you can, make an offering to the goddess, using her sigil and the suggestions earlier in this section.

Haurvatat Sigil

Haurvatat

PART THREE

CHAPTER FIVE

Sample Gratitude Ritual

This basic ritual is ideal for making an offering to a spirit right after pathworking them. The expression of proper gratitude is essential in every magik practice, and it becomes even more significant when the magik starts to take effect.

Set up your altar space. Minimal tools or props.

Items Needed:

Single altar candle
Spirit's sigil or other item connected to the spirit
The offering and offering bowl
Fireproof bowl is this is a daemon spirit
Spare sigil and diabetic lancet if this is a daemon

Summon the spirit using the summoning you used originally, or a variation of it. Daemon summoning is simply saying their ENN three times.

Make the offering. Say the standard phrase: "_______ please accept this humble offering in gratitude for assisting me."

The offering will vary by ritual and spirit. Drop of blood on the sigil of a daemon, otherwise wine or spirits, sweet bread, as used in previous offerings to this spirit.

Close the ritual by dismissing the spirit, usually by saying: "__________, you may depart, go back to your land of mountains and forests, and please come again when I next call upon you."

Again: wait overnight or 24 hrs., then dispose of the offering.

CHAPTER SIX

Wealth Magik

Defining Wealth

Which sequence will you be drawn to? A wealth of family? Being surrounded by cousins, nephews, children and grandchildren? All living in luxury?

In a world driven by material possessions and financial success, the concept of wealth has traditionally been associated with financial abundance. However, true wealth extends far beyond mere monetary value. It encompasses a diverse range of elements that contribute to a fulfilling and meaningful life.

Financial prosperity is undoubtedly an essential aspect of wealth. It provides individuals with the means to fulfill their basic needs, pursue opportunities, and enjoy a certain level of comfort and security. Money enables access to education, healthcare, and other resources that enhance one's quality of life. It is imperative to acknowledge that financial prosperity is not enough for true wealth.

The state of one's physical and mental well-being is a fundamental component of wealth. Without good health, monetary riches lose their value. Wealth is about having the vitality and energy to engage in meaningful activities, enjoy relationships, and pursue personal growth. Investing in self-care, maintaining a balanced lifestyle, and fostering positive mental health are indispensable aspects of true wealth.

Another vital dimension of wealth lies in the quality of our relationships and social connections. Genuine wealth is not measured by the number of material possessions but by the depth and authenticity of our connections with others. Strong relationships provide emotional support, love, and a sense of belonging. They enrich our lives and contribute significantly to our overall well-being.

Wealth is intricately linked to personal fulfillment and finding purpose in life. It is about engaging in activities that align with our passions, values, and strengths. A person pursuing their true calling, whether it be a career, creative endeavor, or philanthropic work, experiences a profound sense of wealth. Material possessions alone cannot fill the void left by a lack of purpose and fulfillment.

Further, wealth encompasses the development and

nurturing of intellectual and emotional intelligence. Intellectual wealth involves acquiring knowledge, continuously learning, and cultivating critical thinking skills. Emotional wealth is about understanding and managing our emotions, as well as developing empathy and compassion towards others. These forms of wealth contribute to personal growth and enable us to navigate life's challenges with resilience and wisdom.

Preparing for wealth magik is like preparing for any other type of magik: Defining your actual desire, digging through the layers, determining which is important to manifesting the desire, and if the desire needs a single ritual or a series of rituals.

And this all can be accomplished by magik.

Don't be turned off by the idea of a sequence of rituals. Magicians throughout history have performed elaborate sequences of rituals towards a single goal.

As with any sequence, we'll look at defeating both internal and external blocks, how to deal with other obstacles, and then writing your petition, including making a sigil for the desire, then a wealth specific ritual template that can be used for all the goddesses in this book, or another deity or daemon of your choosing.

Goddess Wealth magik

Each one of the goddesses in this book can be used for obtaining money and, eventually, acquiring wealth. It's a sequence you might be familiar with if you have my other wealth books, a sequence which begins with defining "wealth", then removing any pre-programmed blocks you may have towards amassing wealth, then removing any external blocks to obtaining wealth, then finally working magik in a specific order to draw wealth to you.

One wealth sequence is designed for material wealth, as defined as a large stock portfolio, bulging bank accounts and acquisition of material things. Another wealth sequence is for surrounding yourself with the wealth of "a loving family". And another sequence is to banish bad luck and draw to you gambling luck as a way to accumulate wealth.

But the first Sequence is about getting money flowing to you right now.

CHAPTER SEVEN

Blocks and Money

Unless you are born into wealth, chances are you might have developed some mental blocks around money.

Here's some non-magikal methods for dealing with mental blocks.

1: Identify the blocks: Start by recognizing and understanding the specific mental blocks that are affecting your income. Common blocks may include self-doubt, fear of failure, limiting beliefs about money, or a lack of confidence in your abilities. Take some time to reflect on your thoughts and emotions surrounding income and identify any negative patterns.

2: Challenge your limiting beliefs: Once you've

identified your limiting beliefs, question their validity. Ask yourself if there is any evidence to support these beliefs or if they are merely assumptions. Replace negative thoughts with positive and empowering affirmations. For example, if you believe that making more money is selfish, reframe it as "I am deserving of financial abundance, and it allows me to make a positive impact on myself and others."

3: Work on self-confidence: Building self-confidence is essential for overcoming mental blocks. Focus on your strengths, achievements, and positive qualities. Take small steps outside your comfort zone to prove to yourself that you are capable of achieving more. Celebrate your successes along the way, no matter how small, to reinforce a positive mindset.

4: Set clear goals: Clearly define your income goals and create a plan to achieve them. Break down your goals into actionable steps and set deadlines for each one. Having a clear direction and plan can help overcome mental blocks and keep you focused on the actions necessary to increase your income.

5: Seek support: Surround yourself with positive and supportive individuals who believe in your potential. Share your goals and aspirations with them, and ask for their encouragement and accountability. Consider working with a mentor, coach, or therapist who specializes in mindset and success to help you overcome mental blocks and develop strategies for improving your income.

6: Continuous learning and personal development: Invest in your personal growth by acquiring new knowledge, developing new skills, and staying updated on trends in your industry. The more you learn and grow, the more confident and valuable you become, increasing your potential for higher income.

7: Practice self-care: Taking care of your mental and physical well-being is crucial. Engage in activities that reduce stress and promote relaxation, such as exercise, meditation, hobbies, or spending time in nature. Prioritize self-care to maintain a positive mindset and reduce the impact of mental blocks on your income.

When it comes to money blocks, it's important to keep in mind that there is often a glimmer of light at the end of the tunnel. However, by utilizing magik, we can strive to ensure that this glimmer of hope doesn't turn out to be a huge, oncoming truck headed straight for you.

Ritual to Marchosias Release Blocks

This ritual to the goddess Marchosias is designed to release or resolve any negative blocks you may have regarding increasing income or blocks from an external source. It's a standard practice to release or remove any blocks prior to working any type of money magik, or income boosting magik.

Blocks come in many different types. There're pre-programmed blocks that happen, quite by accident, when you are younger. These occur when a parent has a discussion (or fight) or money and financial hardships. These types of blocks are often hidden, and takes a bit to remove, as you need to purge them out of your subconscious.

There are blocks that have emerged due to recent events related to finances, for instance, losing one's job or being unable to earn income due to an illness. As a consequence of these events, obstacles have surfaced which must be dealt with and resolved.

Besides working the steps in the previous section, you can also petition the Goddess Marchosias to help you remove these internal blocks and any external blocks.

External blocks can form due to work condition, your supervisors, cuts in pay from an uncaring company, plus many, many more. Some external issues, such as economic factors, such as recessions, inflation, or market fluctuations, can affect income potential. During economic downturns, job opportunities may be limited, and businesses may struggle, resulting in lower incomes for individuals.

We can address these blocks by giving you an advantage over competitors in your job sector, drawing more clients when you are self-employed, or just starting to be self-employed.

Sometimes you can be the target of intended energy that blocks your income. There are various reasons why someone might try to stop your income-generating endeavors, such as jealousy or a need to exert control over you. In these instances, you can petition Marchosias to remove those people and their energy.

In dealing with internal blocks, I suggest you run two rituals, separated by at least 24 hours. If you wish to work within astrological energy, plan to work these rituals nearly before the new moon, when the moon's energies will aid you in eliminating these blocks. Ritual one 72 hours before the new moon, with ritual two 48 hours before the new moon. Consult one of the many moon calendars available online.

Goddess Blocks Ritual One

The first of two suggested rituals to deal with blocks.

First, we start with the petition. Let's take a look at a

petition template for this purpose. You will need to adjust it for your own circumstances.

"Goddess Marchosias, I ask you to assist me in recognizing my mental blocks in allowing income to flow to me. I ask that you gently help me remove those blocks, and that solutions for my situation present themselves."

The ritual is straightforward, and you summon the Goddess aspect of Marchosias

Items Needed:

Goddess Sigil

Orange Blocks Remove candle

Yellow candles to open communication

Petition

Offering and offering bowl

Cast the circle as previously instructed.

Once this is done, face your altar and look at Marchosias's sigil. Take a deep breath and begin to let go of any tension or stress, allowing yourself to ease into the alpha head-space.

Think about the magik you are about to perform. Visualize at this time the goddess working to assist you in manifesting your desire. Trace over the sigil using your finger, or a black ink pen.

Now, say the following to properly summon Marchosias:

Goddess of Change, Goddess Marchosias, hear my call;

Goddess of Divine power and influence;

Goddess of Wealth and Power, Goddess Marchosias;

Speed to me and join with me in my space.

Goddess Marchosias, I have a request:

At this point, read your petition.

Once you have read your petition, take a few moments to visualize again the results of your desire manifesting. Then, (this is optional) you may burn the petition in the fireproof bowl to seal the pact. While the pact paper burns, say:

As this petition is burned, a pact is formed, and it will be executed quickly harming no one.

Now, continue with the offering. Pick up your offering, and say:

Goddess Marchosias, to express my deepest gratitude for your working on my behalf, I offer to you

this humble (your offering).

Place the offering on her sigil, and it's time to close the ritual.

You may close this ritual in any way that suits you, or you can simply say:

This ritual is done, and I ask that you leave in peace, and come again when I next call.

Allow the offering to stay on Marchosias's Goddess sigil overnight, then dispose of it as I instructed earlier.

Next, prepare for ritual two.

Goddess Blocks Ritual Two

Once again, we start with the petition. Let's take a look at a petition template for this purpose. You will need to adjust it for your own circumstances.

"Goddess Marchosias, I ask you to assist me in negating and removing any energy directed at me from another person, shield me from their energy, remove their influence and allow me to move forward!"

One possible negative outcome to this is if your living situation is precarious, such as having to live with someone who's blocking you, this might trigger a housing crisis and force you to move. In case you are faced with any of those circumstances, it's imperative to plan for a move and update your petition to include provisions for the funds required to relocate promptly and smoothly.

The ritual itself is a copy of the previous ritual, except for candle colors.

Items Needed:

Goddess Sigil

Reversed Red Removal candle*

Petition

Offering and offering bowl

Cast the circle as previously instructed.

Once this is done, face your altar and look at Marchosias's sigil. Take a deep breath and begin to let go of any tension or stress, allowing yourself to ease into the alpha head-space.

Think about the magik you are about to perform. Visualize at this time the goddess working to assist you in manifesting your desire. Trace over the sigil using your finger, or a black ink pen.

Now, say the following to properly summon Marchosias:

Goddess of Change, Goddess Marchosias, hear my call;

Goddess of Divine power and influence;

Goddess of Wealth and Power, Goddess Marchosias;

Speed to me and join with me in my space.

Goddess Marchosias, I have a request:

At this point, read your petition.

Once you have read your petition, take a few moments to visualize again the results of your desire manifesting. Then, (this is optional) you may burn the petition in the fireproof bowl to seal the pact. While the pact paper burns, say:

As this petition is burned, a pact is formed, and it will be executed quickly harming no one.

Now, continue with the offering. Pick up your offering, and say:

Goddess Marchosias, to express my deepest gratitude for your working on my behalf, I offer to you this humble (your offering).

Place the offering on her sigil, and it's time to close the ritual.

You may close this ritual in any way that suits you, or you can simply say:

This ritual is done, and I ask that you leave in peace, and come again when I next call.

Allow the offering to stay on Marchosias's Goddess sigil overnight, then dispose of it as I instructed earlier.

(*Reversed Red candles - sometimes you can obtain one from a magic store, and sometimes you can just make one. Take a regular red stick candle and cut the top so that it's a flat surface. Turn the candle over, and carve a "new top" to expose the wick. To use, place in a sturdy holder and light the exposed wick.)

CHAPTER EIGHT

Money Ritual for Quick Cash

Goddess Ritual

This can be worked for any of the goddesses in this book. All you have to do it adjust the petition where indicated and use the correct sigils in the ritual.

Suggested petition: **"Goddess ________, I come to you today and ask that you assist me in manifesting a large sum of money, in (your country's money system - e.g., "dollars" if in the US), and this continues in ever-increasing amounts. I ask that this be done swiftly and without harm to anyone."**

Once you have the petition crafted, it's time for the ritual. If you follow any astrological magik restraints, then execute this ritual shortly after a new moon, on a Sunday or Thursday, the traditional days of business and money.

The ritual outline is the same for all the goddesses. Adjust as needed for the particular goddess you have chosen. In this example, I'm using Gremory.

This goddess ritual is pretty straightforward. Since you are dealing with a goddess form, elaborate precautions shouldn't be necessary (see Chapter One on preparations), some protection might be needed, depending on your situation. As I keep a permanent altar space, I only have to purify once in a while, versus when I used my bedroom which was frequently intruded by the other occupants of the house for various reasons.

Items needed:

- Altar candles in green for money luck
- Goddess sigil
- Dedicated goddess candle, Silver or White
- Offering and Offering bowl
- Incense and incense burner
- Petition and fireproof bowl

Begin by lighting the candles and making sure you

have everything you need on your altar.

Lights go off.

Next, casting the traditional circle and getting rid of any outside negative energies hanging around your space. You can start by fumigating the area with incense. Then face each direction and trace out your circle. (See appendix on circle casting in a Goddess Ritual)

Once this is done, face your altar and look at Gremory's sigil. Take a deep breath and begin to let go of any tension or stress, allowing yourself to ease into the alpha head-space.

Think about the magik you are about to perform. Visualize at this time the goddess working to assist you in manifesting your desire.

Now, say the following to properly summon Gremory:

Goddess of the celestial sphere, hear me now.

Goddess Gremory, goddess of wealth, family, and health.

Hear me, Goddess Gremory, you who are timeless and eternal,

Grace me with your presence.

Join with me now, here in my space,

Hear me, Goddess Gremory, please listen to my

prayers and/or petition:

At this point, read your petition.

Once you have read your petition, take a few moments to visualize again the results of your desire manifesting. Then, (this is optional) you may burn the petition in the fireproof bowl to seal the pact. While the pact paper burns, say:

As this petition is burned, a pact is formed, and it will be executed quickly harming no one.

Now, continue with the offering. Pick up your offering, and say:

Goddess Gremory, to express my deepest gratitude for your working on my behalf, I offer to you this humble (your offering).

Place the offering on her sigil, and it's time to close the ritual.

You may close this ritual in any way that suits you, or you can simply say:

This ritual is done, and I ask that you leave in peace, and come again when I next call.

Allow the offering to stay on Gremory's Goddess sigil overnight, then dispose of it as I instructed earlier.

Daemonic Ritual

You might decide to work with daemonic forms of Gremory or Marchosias, as they will work pretty quickly when petitioned.

In this example, we'll use Marchosias as she's adept at finding new sources of income in this form.

Your petition can be worded as follows. Remember, you can modify this as needed for your situation.

"Marchosias, I humbly request your assistance in significantly boosting my current income. I ask that this is done swiftly and without harm to anyone."

Since you are dealing with her in her daemonic form, protection might be needed, depending on your situation. As I keep a permanent altar space, I only have to purify once in a while, versus when I used my bedroom which was frequently intruded by the other occupants of the house for various reasons. Consult the appendix for a method of casting a circle when working with daemonic forms of these goddesses.

Items needed:

Altar candles

Two of Marchosias' sigils

Dedicated daemonic candle, gold or yellow

Silver or Green candle for money

Diabetic lancet

Incense and incense burner

Petition and fireproof bowl

Begin by lighting the candles and making sure you have everything you need on your altar.

Lights go off.

Next, casting the traditional circle and getting rid of any outside negative energies hanging around your space. You can start by fumigating the area with incense. Then face each direction and trace out your circle. (See appendix on circle casting)

Once this is done, face your altar and look at Marchosias's sigil. Take a deep breath and begin to let go of any tension or stress, allowing yourself to ease into the alpha head-space.

Think about the magik you are about to perform. Visualize at this time the her in her daemonic form working to assist you in manifesting your desire. Trace over the sigil using your finger, or a black ink pen.

Now, say the following to properly summon Marchosias:

Es Na Ayer Marchosias Secore

Es Na Ayer Marchosias Secore

Es Na Ayer Marchosias Secore

Daemon of change, daemon of hidden wealth,

Daemon of protection, daemon of courage,

Speed to me and join with me in my space.

Marchosias, I have a request:

At this point, read your petition.

Once you have read your petition, take a few moments to visualize again the results of your desire manifesting. Then, (this is optional) you may burn the petition in the fireproof bowl to seal the pact. While the pact paper burns, say:

As this petition is burned, a pact is formed, and it will be executed quickly harming no one.

Now, continue with the offering. Prick a finger using the diabetic lancet, place a single drop of blood onto one of her sigils, then touch it to a candle flame, and drop it into the fireproof bowl and allow it to be totally consumed by fire, all while saying:

Marchosias, please accept a drop of my essence as an offering in gratitude for you attending to my petition in a timely manner.

Place the offering on her sigil, and it's time to close the ritual.

You may close this ritual in any way that suits you, or you can simply say:

This ritual is done, and I ask that you leave in peace, and come again when I next call.

The ritual is complete.

CHAPTER NINE

Increasing Wealth Goddess Ritual

It's best to use a goddess to increase one's wealth. The first step in the long-term sequence is performing another round of block removal rituals, followed by executing this particular ritual. You can repeat this sequence monthly until tangible results begin to manifest. At that time, work a gratitude ritual immediately.

Use the same timing, Block Ritual One, approximately 72 hours prior to the New Moon, followed 24 hours later by Block Ritual Two.

Then commence this ritual. If you follow any astrological restraints on magik, plan this ritual for the first Thursday after the New Moon. Repeat on a monthly cycle as needed.

You have the liberty to select any of the goddesses

mentioned in this book and make the required alterations in the ritual that is presented below. The offering should be dark wine, or very sweet bread or cake.

We'll start with the petition statement. We're looking to increase income to the point it transforms into wealth, assuming we're going for financial wealth. In this sample, I'm addressing Goddess Haurvatat.

"Oh, great Goddess Haurvatat, who is known for her blessings in wealth and family matters, I humbly beseech you to grant me your divine favor and increase my income manifold. Please bless me with a financial stability that lasts not just for days, but for weeks and months to come."

Adjust this petition if using one of the other goddesses.

Goddess Ritual

Items Needed:

Altar candle in white

Goddess Sigil

Wealth candle in gold.

Petition

Fire proof bowl

Offering and offering bowl

We begin by casting a standard circle and ejecting any negative energies:

Face north, aim a finger, a wand, or a crystal point at a spot on the floor. Imagine light, gold or yellow, flowing from your hand. Slowly, trace out a circle on the floor. This defines the magik circle.

Once this is done, face north again and cast out any negative energies by saying:

Only that which I invite is allowed to remain in this sacred spot. All others must depart now!

Spend a moment or two visualizing the outcome of your desire manifesting. Take your time. With Haurvatat, see her helping make this manifest.

Next, pick up her sigil and trace along its design, activating the image.

Now, we call on Haurvatat:

Ahura Mazda spoke unto the lands, and saying:

"I created for the faithful the help, the enjoyments, the comforts, and the pleasures of Haurvatat."

I call now on Goddess Haurvatat to join with

me in this sacred space,

I offer to thee libations and offerings to sate thy appetite

Haurvatat - hear my pleas:

Read your petition at this point.

Haurvatat, I thank you for attending to my plea, and I now offer to you this ________.

I ask for your blessings and assistance in manifesting my desire! Please enchant this (candle/sigil/etc.) to quickly draw to me my desire, and with your help, my desire will arrive swiftly!

Pause again, and visualize your desire/manifestation having already happened.

To close the ritual, say: **Haurvatat, again I thank thee for your presence here. This ritual is now complete and you may depart in peace, and come again when I next call upon you.**

As with the other rituals, leave the offering in place overnight, then dispose of as instructed earlier.

Once this is done, follow up with a repeat of this sequence after a month.

CHAPTER TEN

Goddess Love Magik

Each one of the goddesses in this book can be used for love or family magik, the same as with the wealth ritual sequence.

Love is just as difficult as money/wealth magik. Longing for a specific person can be challenging as there may be blocks that need to be overcome and the target's cooperation is essential for the magik to work. If I may, let me recommend that you focus on general attraction magic instead of targeting a specific person. This is because when you concentrate exclusively on one individual, it may cause you to disregard other potential matches, ultimately resulting in more heartbreak and mental anguish.

There is a unique magik ritual to Marchosias to uncover who might be your ideal partner. This leverages her unique powers of divination. Sometimes, due to circumstances governed by our spirit guides, this person may be kept hidden from you, and no amount of magik would reveal this person. Thus, if you get nothing asking Marchosias for this person's face, you can then work a general attraction and glamor magik so that when this person is revealed, they'll be as attracted to you as you will be attracted to them.

Then again, this person might be having their own issues and unable to enter into a relationship until a time in the future when they're more emotionally prepared for a relationship. They may have gotten out of a relationship and haven't processed the grief which comes from an ended relationship, or they may be unable to get go. If this is the case, little magik will work on them, except for a ritual that could assist them in healing.

I am approached on a weekly basis for help in these matters. People who put themselves through emotional pain because they have become fixated on someone who isn't available. Whenever someone faces such a dilemma, I often suggest they try a glamor ritual, which can help them attract someone new while also letting go of their fixation that is causing more harm than good. Such a ritual is presented here as one option.

Personally, I spent a great deal of my time during my twenties practicing different types of magic that were centered around love and relationships. I have confessed to this in my Lilith book, but I can admit to fixating on someone who was either unable or unwilling to be with me, and I can attest to the emotional torture I endured. I discovered a small ritual to assist me in getting over someone, and I'll have it here.

If I had known to work with Marchosias at that time, I might have been able to fathom out who to expect and when.

Glamor Goddess Ritual

Like in my Lilith book, I suggest this magick, along with any other magick, to attract someone to you. Projecting this magick will go a long way in assisting you in attracting someone.

This works on the principle of "Like Attracting Like". I discovered something interesting back in the late 1980s. When I was just married, I must have been projecting the aura of love and glamor, because I was attracting some very attractive, and interested, women. The reason behind this can be attributed to the Law of Attraction, which is a peculiar universal law.

This magick will work off this principal. By projecting glamor, love, sexuality, you attract that to you.

Apart from its primary function, it is worth mentioning that the Glamor Ritual has the potential to project charisma and can be used for the same. This can be particularly useful in situations where you may need to enchant large groups of people, whether it's delivering an important speech or running for a political office. Actors can use this power when auditioning to help sway the casting people to hire you for a part in either a play or movie.

This is a simple physical ritual.

The petition is quite straightforward, and the suggested wording is as follows: **"Divine Goddess, I humbly**

implore you to make adjustments to my energy and create a radiant aura of glamor that will enable me to exude a warm glow of love that will be visible to all those around me."

You can also create a sigil for this, and perhaps wear it as a charm or carry on a key-chain. I suggest the statement be: "(Goddess) has given me the aura of glamor and desirability."

In this example, I am using the Goddess Gremory. Feel free to substitute any of the other goddesses, making changes to this ritual.

Items needed:

Altar Candle

Goddess Sigil

Your petition

Any Glamor Aura sigil you created

Incense

Pink ritual candle

Offering

Offering bowl

Any oils necessary

Steps:

We begin by casting a standard circle and ejecting any

negative energies:

Face north, aim a finger, a wand, or a crystal point at a spot on the floor. Imagine light, gold or yellow, flowing from your hand. Slowly, trace out a circle on the floor. This defines the magik circle.

Once this is done, face north again and cast out any negative energies by saying:

Only that which I invite is allowed to remain in this sacred spot. All others must depart now!

Spend a moment or two visualizing the outcome of your desire manifesting. Take your time. With Gremory, see her helping make this manifest.

Next, pick up her sigil and trace along its design, activating the image.

Invocation to Goddess Gremory

Goddess of the celestial sphere, hear me now.

Goddess Gremory, goddess of wealth, family, and health.

Hear me, Goddess Gremory, you who are timeless and eternal,

Grace me with your presence.

Join with me now, here in my space,

Hear me, Goddess Gremory, please listen to my prayers and/or petition:

At this point, read your petition.

Once you have read your petition, take a few moments to visualize again the results of your desire manifesting. Then, (this is optional) you may burn the petition in the fireproof bowl to seal the pact. While the pact paper burns, say:

As this petition is burned, a pact is formed, and it will be executed quickly harming no one.

Now, continue with the offering. Pick up your offering, and say:

Goddess Gremory, to express my deepest gratitude for your working on my behalf, I offer to you this humble (your offering).

Place the offering on her sigil, and it's time to close the ritual.

You may close this ritual in any way that suits you, or you can simply say:

This ritual is done, and I ask that you leave in peace, and come again when I next call.

Allow the offering to stay on Gremory's Goddess sigil overnight, then dispose of it as I instructed earlier.

Letting Go, Moving On

Sometimes, a relationship ends. This means a period for grief, as with any ended relationship, then it's time to move along. Sometimes, this can be difficult. Especially the healing.

This brief ritual is intended to ask a goddess for help in healing. The focus is on a usual healing energy, although the target is not physical afflictions, but rather, the emotional wounds of the heart that we aim to heal.

For this, we'll look to the most sympathetic of the goddesses, Skadi. With her gentle and calming demeanor, she exudes a soft energy that is very comforting. Additionally, her emphasis on family values brings with it the necessary empathy to provide you with the support you need to heal your emotional wounds.

The petition should be worded in the following manner: "**Goddess Skadi, mighty huntress, protector, and healer, I ask that you lend your healing powers to ease the sorrow that has taken hold of my heart.**"

Of course, change that statement as needed for your situation.

Ritual to Skadi

Although this one can be worked as a simple pathworking, you may find a full ritual will give you the energy to begin healing.

You will need:

Altar candles in white or silver

Goddess sigil

Dedicated goddess candle, Silver or White

Offering and Offering bowl

Incense and incense burner

Petition and fireproof bowl

Since she doesn't pose a threat to anyone summoning her, we use a simpler circle casting compared to some daemons. Cast a circle using golden light to facilitate the communicated between you and the goddess.

Once this is done, face north and calm your mind. A couple of deep breaths, and visualize your desire manifesting with the help of this goddess. Take your time.

Pick up her sigil. Trace the lines with your finger, activating the sigil.

Now, the suggested summoning:

Great Skadi, Goddess of Winter, I come before

you to seek your blessings.

Goddess Skadi, I ask that you now join with me and hear my request,

You have comforted thousands of petitioners for thousands of years,

Goddess of the Hunt, Goddess of hidden wealth,

I ask now that you join with me.

Again, pause a few moments, and see if you can detect her arrival. Take another deep breath, and then read your petition.

Pause again, and visualize the results of your petition manifesting. Take as long as you need.

Try now to visualize Skadi near you, dressed in furs, a hunting bow on her back. She'll be nodding and agreeing to assist you in manifesting your desire.

Once you are satisfied you have visualized enough, give her the initial offering.

Goddess Skadi, in gratitude for listening and acting upon my desire, I offer to you this humble (your offering). Thank you again for being with me!

Now it's time to end the ritual. I usually say something like this:

Goddess, our time together is now at an end. You may depart, go back to your land of mountains and forests, and please come again when I next call upon you.

That's it. The ritual is completed.

Who Might It Be?

The ritual involves utilizing her extraordinary abilities to help you identify your potential next partner or determine whether your current partner is the right fit for you (although, if you are doubtful about your current relationship, it may be worth examining the reasons behind those doubts).

Although you are free to petition her as a daemon, it works best if you use her goddess invocation for this ritual.

It is crucial that we take great care in wording the petition for this matter. It could be necessary for you to find a way around the barriers put up by guides who firmly believe what is best for you, and establish a means for her to pass on this information to you, in case you lack the ability to listen to the spirit. To this end, I suggest using a pendulum with one of the better answer circles, found in the appendix and on my website as a download.

In order for the petition to be effective, it is recommended that it be worded as follows: **"Goddess Marchosias, I humbly ask for your guidance in revealing my intended partner. May you grant me the vision of their image, the knowledge of the circumstances of our meeting, and your divine guidance in leading me to this person."**

You will need:

Altar candles and Marchosias' candle in yellow or gold

Discovery purple candle

Offering and Offering bowl

Incense and incense burner

Petition and fireproof bowl

Pendulum and Answer Circle

Begin by lighting the candles and making sure you have everything you need on your altar.

Now, the lights go off.

Next, casting the traditional circle and getting rid of any outside negative energies hanging around your space. You can start by fumigating the area with incense. Then face each direction and trace out your circle. (See appendix on circle casting in a Goddess Ritual)

Once this is done, face your altar and look at Marchosias's sigil. Take a deep breath and begin to let go of any tension or stress, allowing yourself to ease into the alpha head-space.

Think about the magik you are about to perform. Visualize at this time the goddess working to assist you in manifesting your desire. Trace over the sigil using your finger, or a black ink pen.

Now, say the following to properly summon

Marchosias:

Goddess of Change, Goddess Marchosias, hear my call;

Goddess of Divine power and influence;

Goddess of Discovery, Goddess of Divination

Speed to me and join with me in my space.

Goddess Marchosias, I have a request!

At this point, read your petition.

Once you have read your petition, take a few moments to visualize again the results of your desire manifesting. Then, (this is optional) you may burn the petition in the fireproof bowl to seal the pact. While the pact paper burns, say:

Once the petition is set on fire, a pact will be formed and it will be executed without any delay or harm to anyone.

Now, continue with the offering. Pick up your offering, and say:

Goddess Marchosias, to express my deepest gratitude for your working on my behalf, I offer to you this humble (your offering).

Place the offering on her sigil, and it's time to close the ritual.

You may close this ritual in any way that suits you, or you can simply say:

> **This ritual is done, and I ask that you leave in peace, and come again when I next call.**

Allow the offering to stay on Marchosias's Goddess sigil overnight, then dispose of it as I instructed earlier.

Keep a notepad next to your bed, for the revelations might come to you in your dreams. To assist you in recalling your dreams, I suggest you locate some self-hypnosis audios on this subject.

Love Rituals

This ritual has been designed with the specific goal of enabling you to engage the necessary magik that will ultimately help you to attract a partner.

This isn't a sequence. However, the sequence can be done using this magik. Run a Let Go ritual. Then the Glamor Ritual. Next, run this ritual.

There are two sections where you will need to customize the ritual. Is there a specific person you desire? Or is this simply "Attract my perfect partner" ritual? That's up to you. However, caution is advised when attempting to attract a specific person. There's great risk to your own emotional well-being if the person of your attention is unwilling, or unable, to return your affection. When this is the case, no amount of magik will cause them to suddenly turn towards you unless they're already attracted to you. In those cases, it's best to see if you can remove the obstacles preventing the relationship. It's in these cases you should think about working a blocks removal ritual, and modify it to target those obstacles.

Which goddess is best at love magik? Any of the goddesses in this book can work very strong love magik. Except the targeted love magik, these rituals do not require any special props, nor do they need you to mix up a special drink to cause your target to suddenly turn to you. Love magick can be performed with specific conditions, but it is important to keep in mind that placing too many conditions may lead to a longer manifestation period as it could present obstacles for the goddess. This ritual is designed to bring to you someone – but not anyone in particular.

Thus, you should request that the Goddess bring you someone who is suitable, available (physically and emotionally). Then you need to be alert to the subtle signals of what actions to do to make sure you encounter this person. It does no good to ask for a lover and sit on the couch watching Lifetime movies and expect that person to be delivered to your doorstep! (Unless the person is a delivery person!)

Of the four goddesses in this book, I have always felt that Lady Haurvatat has powerful love magik, and Skadi is great for family magik, protection of loved ones, and for strength to unborn babies, to allow for successful childbirth.

For this generic ritual, we'll be using Lady Haurvatat.

General Love Bring

Now, on to the ritual.

This ritual should be performed on a Friday, the day of Venus.

Orient your altar so that it faces *north*

Altar items:

- Image of the goddess
- offering bowl
- fireproof bowl
- 2 candles (white or white & black)
- One PINK candle
- Incense (floral or plain Frankincense)
- Offerings (heavy cream or milk & honey)
- The petition written out in magik ink.

Light a candle. Douse the room's light, cast the circle, breathe, and calm yourself. Stand facing your altar (and facing north). Light the other candle. Start the incense.

Invocation of Lady Haurvatat

Ahura Mazda spoke unto the lands, and saying:

"I created for the faithful the help, the enjoyments, the comforts, and the pleasures of

Haurvatat."

I call now on Goddess Haurvatat to join with me in this sacred space,

I offer to thee libations and offerings to sate thy appetite

Join with me, in my soul and in my heart!

I ask that you be present and listen to my request.

Read from your prepared petition.

I ask now that you bless this candle to bring to me what I desire!

Light the PINK candle

Go into a daydream about who this person might be, but focus on how you will FEEL when meeting this person. Visualize the results. Go into as much detail as possible. Hold those feelings as the goddess begins to work her magick.

Lady Haurvatat! Please accept this humble offering, given freely to you in gratitude for listening to my request!

Place the offering near or on top of her sigil.

When this is done and when you feel you have meditated long enough on the issue, speak the following words to allow the Goddess to depart:

Lady Haurvatat!

I grant you leave to depart, having heard my petition.

I thank you and wish you speed on your return journey to the land of the three rivers.

At this point, meditate a moment, then set the petition on fire, holding it over the fire proof bowl.

After the material has been completely burned to ash, it is important to ensure that it has been fully reduced to ash by stirring the ashes. Once this has been done, take the ashes outside and find a natural location such as a bush or grass, and cast the ashes into nature. This will allow the ashes to return to the earth and complete the natural cycle of life and death.

The ritual is done.

Extinguish the candles except for the PINK candle. Allow it to SAFELY burn out completely. Allow the incense to completely burn.

Appendix

Sigils

Gremory Goddess

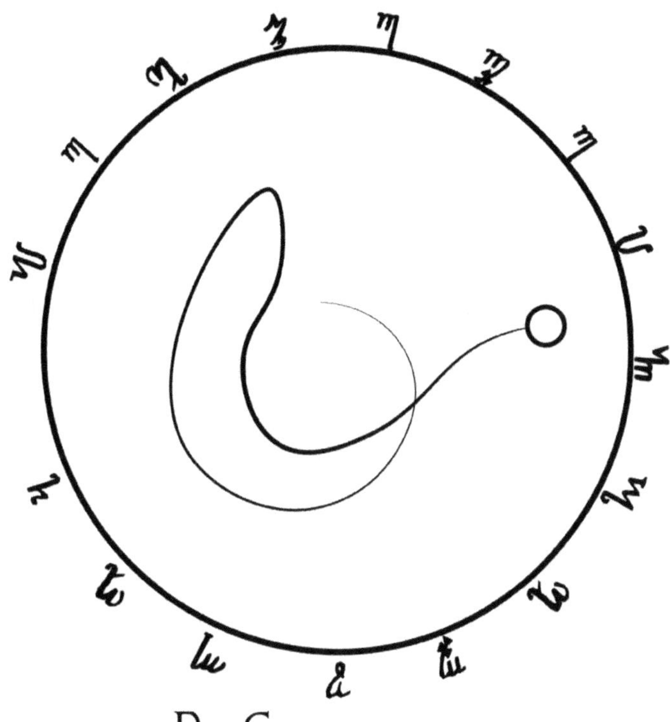

Gremory Daemoness

Gremory

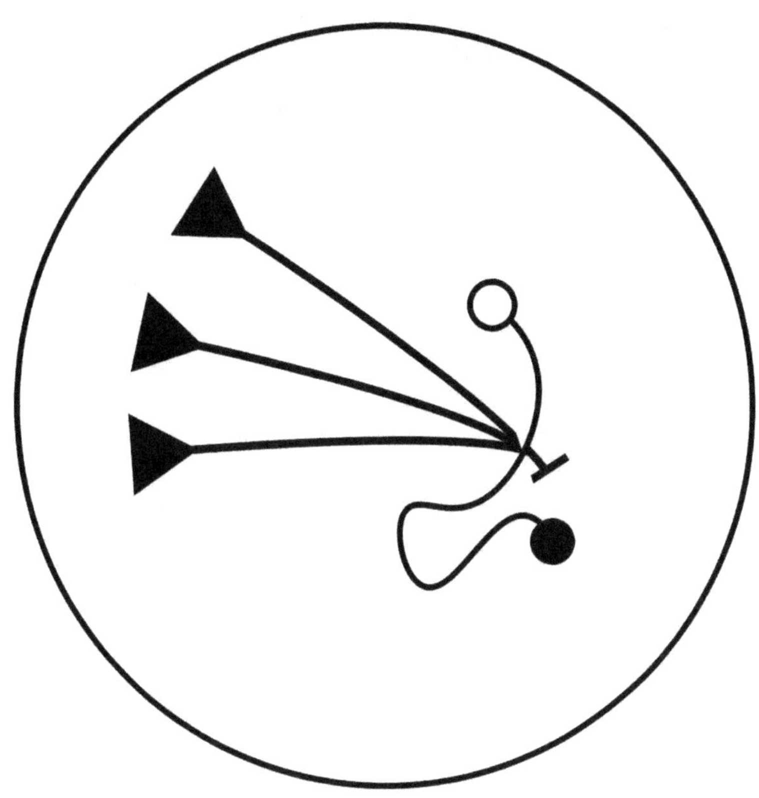

Goddess Skadi

Skadi

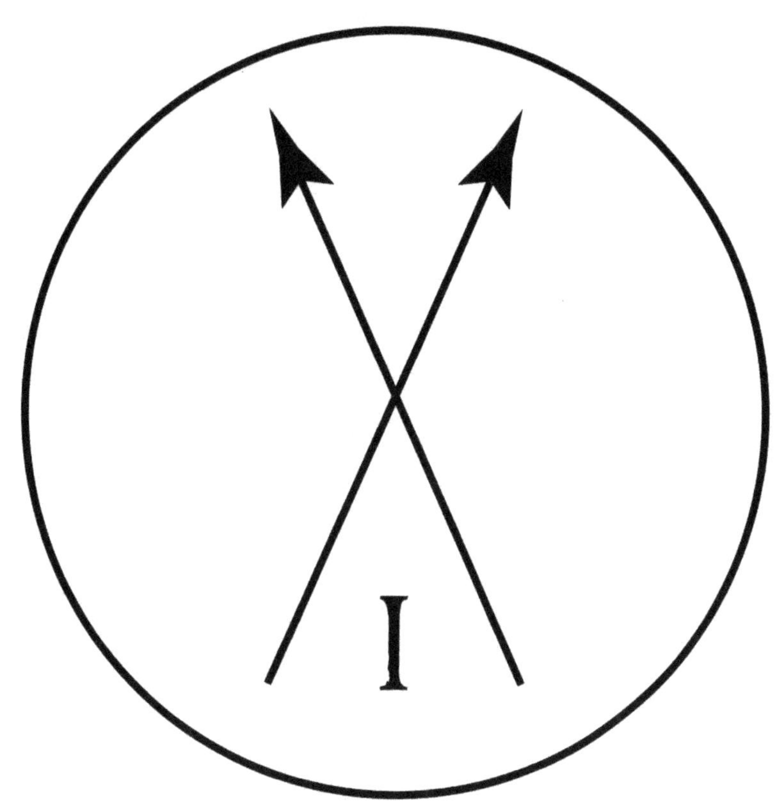

Goddess Marchosias

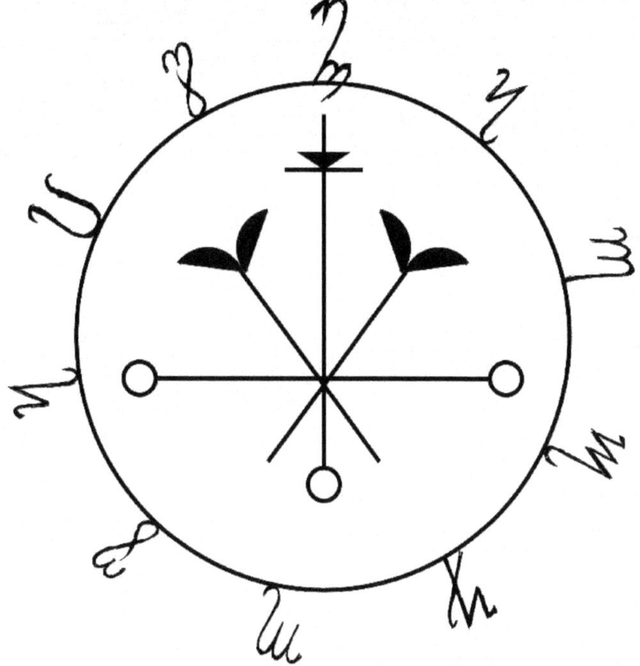

Goddess Haurvatat

Goddess magik Circle Casting

With my type of magik, a circle is used less for protection, and more for opening up a channel through which you make contact with the energy of the universe and the particular god you wish to summon.

If you work in an area known for negativity, or you have a temporary space, this circle will also allow you to sanctify the space and eject any negative energies.

If this is the case, and you are just beginning, I then suggest using the banishing ritual while casting your circle. I'll cover both in this chapter.

Make sure you have space to walk all around your table/altar.

Get the incense going, and all ritual candles are lit (save the one candle for your desire).

Make sure to mark the directions, as you start with facing north in this method and then walk CLOCK-wise around your altar.

As you walk, aim the athame, crystal point or a finger at the ground, defining the circle.

Imagine golden light, like liquid sunlight, shooting out of the pointing device, and leaving a visible trail in the floor.

When you get to the starting point, stop and face north.

In my mind, I will see the circle of light on the floor expand and flow upwards, creating a cylinder which goes up into the space above you, creating a pillar of energy. Make sure to see this fully in your mind.

Say: "I have now cast this circle. I now banish all non-positive energies from this space!"

Sweep in a circle and, when facing WEST, act as if you are tossing away the negative energies.

When finished in Ritual, I simply say "This ritual is over. This circle may now dissolve,"

Alternative Circle Casting ritual

Another method, which uses a summoning of beings from each direction, and this particular circle casting is widely used by people who following the Wiccan way of ritual.

1. Place four (4) makers to represent north, south, east and west. (These can be anything, even pencils for the witch in hiding.)

2. Stand in the center of the circle and say:

I cast this circle to enhance my energies and to protect me from all harm. I cast this circle and only the most balanced and positive energies may enter.

3. Now the caster is to call upon the elements:

I call upon the guardians and the watchtowers of the north/east/south/west elements of earth/air/fire/water. Guard and guide me. Hail and welcome.

4. Now call on the Lord and Lady by saying:

I call upon the Lord and Lady and the Great Spirit to lend their energies and protect me.

5. When finished with your ritual, simply say:

My work is done, Thank you elements of earth, air, fire and water; Great Spirit and Lord and Lady, may my magic disperse into the universe and may my circle end.

That's pretty much it for casting your circle. Don't get too caught up in what needs to be said, as long as you hold your intent on the task at hand and establishing a channel of communication for your work.

Copy this down by hand so you can have it handy when in your space for a ritual.

Daemonic magik Circle Casting (available online from multiple websites)

Traditional Daemonic invocations involve facing each cardinal direction, summoning the guardian of that direction, then drawing a small sigil in the air. I will first trace out my circle, using a crystal wand, while visualizing golden energy being emitted from the crystal wand, which then defines the circle.

Make sure you know which direction is which in your space. Use a compass app and make a note of each direction. Begin drawing the circle by facing east, the direction of the rising sun, which is also the direction guarded by Lucifer Morningstar.

Face East - invoke Lucifer (Air) with his ENN:

Renich Tasa Uberaca Biasa Icar, Lucifer

Face South - invoke Flereous (Fire) with his ENN:

Ganic Tasa fubin, Flereous

Face West - invoke Leviathan (Water) with his ENN:

Jedan Tasa hoet naca, Leviathan

Face North - invoke Belial (Earth) with his ENN:

Lirach Tasa Vefa Wehlic, Belial.

Look up and invoke Satan with his ENN:

Ave Satanis, Tasa reme laris Satan

As you face the direction, after summoning the daemonic guardian, you can also trace out a pentacle in the air, or the traditional “ZD” sigil:

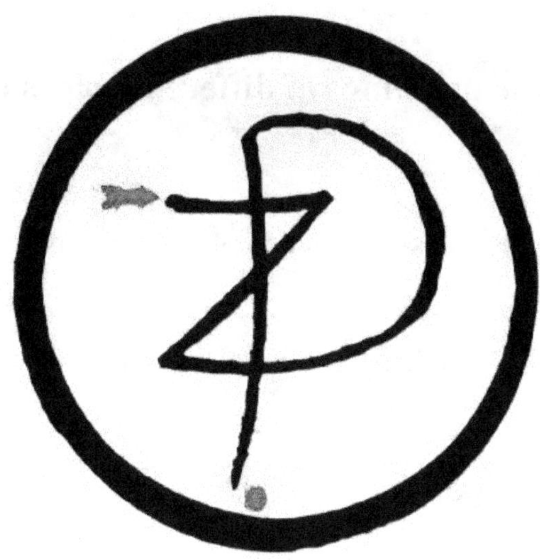

Begin where the red arrow indicates, and in one fluid movement, draw the Z then D, ending below the sigil as shown.

You are now ready to begin the ritual.

Here are the meanings of different colors in general:

White candles-Destruction of negative energy, peace, truth and purity

Purple candles- Spiritual awareness, wisdom, tranquility

Lavender Candles– Intuition, Paranormal, Peace, Healing

Blue and Deep Blue Candles– Meditation, Healing, Forgiveness, Inspiration, Fidelity, Happiness, and opening lines of Communication.

Green Candles– Money, Fertility, Luck, Abundance, Health (not to be used when diagnosed with Cancer), Success

Rose and Pink Colored Candles– Positive self-love, friendship, harmony, joy

Yellow Candles- Realizing and manifesting thoughts, opening up communication, confidence, bringing plans into action, creativity, intelligence, mental clarity, clairvoyance.

Orange Candles– Joy, energy, education, strength attraction, stimulation

Red or Deep red Candles– Passion, energy, love, lust, relationships, sex, vitality, courage.

Black Candles– Protection, absorption and

destruction of negative energy and also repelling negative energy from others

Silver candle– Goddess or feminine energy, remove negativity, psychic development, money

Gold candle– Male energy, Solar energy, fortune, spiritual attainment, money.

Candle colors and Days:

Sunday– Gold or yellow candles

Monday– Silver, Grey or White

Tuesday-Red

Wednesday-Purple

Thursday– Blue

Friday-Green

Saturday– Black or Purple

Candle colors and healing purposes:

Allergies- Violet

Anxiety- Rose

Colds- Green/violet

Depression-Orange/Indigo/Rose

Insomnia-Blue

Indigestion-Yellow

Fever-Blue

Headaches-Green/blue

Diabetes-Yellow

White

The Goddess

Higher Self

Purity

Peace

Virginity

(substitutes any other color)

Black

Binding

Shapeshifting

Protection

Repels Negativity

Brown

Special Favors

To Influence Friendships

Silver

The Goddess

Astral energy

Female energy

Telepathy

Clairvoyance

Intuition

Dreams

<u>Purple</u>

Third Eye

Psychic Ability

Hidden Knowledge

To Influence People in High Places

Spiritual Power

<u>Blue</u>

Element of Water

Wisdom

Protection

Calm

Good Fortune

Opening Blocked Communication

Spiritual Inspiration

<u>Green</u>

The Element of Earth

Physical Healing

Monetary success

Mother Earth

Tree and Plant Magic

Growth

Personal Goals

Pink

Affection

Romance

Affection

Caring

Nurturing

Planetary Good Will

Red

Element of Fire

Passion

Strength

Fast action

Career Goals

Lust

Driving Force

Survival

Blood of the Moon

Orange

General Success

Property Deals

Legal matters

Justice

Selling

Copper

Professional Growth

Business Fertility

Career Maneuvers

Passion

Money Goals

Gold

The God

Promote Winning

Power of the Male

Happiness

Yellow

The Element of Air

Intelligence

The Sun

Memory

Logical Imagination

To Accelerate Learning

To Break Mental Blocks

ABOUT THE AUTHOR

Dave is an author of adult fantasy (The Furies series) as well as author of occult books about magick.

David began working ritual magick back in the 1970s. He took a brief break, then used the power of this magick to create a photography career which took him to Los Angeles and work as a photographer for multiple magazines.

David has studied magick in all forms, and in 2018, released a three-part magick instruction course in High Magick. Thousands of students have benefited from David's unique teaching style, making ceremonial magick accessible to everyone.

This book on Goddesses is number 8 in his High Magick Series.

Dave also has a series on Grecian Magick, exploring the aspects of ceremonial magick with the gods and goddesses of ancient Greece.

Dave's Facebook Page:

https://www.facebook.com/DavePsychic/

Secrets of Magick Facebook Group:

https://www.facebook.com/groups/secretsofmagick

Join the Grecian Magick Facebook group!

https://www.facebook.com/groups/grecianmagick

Dave's webpage, book readings and his services:

https://davepsychic.com

Then his e-learning website for magik classes

https://highmagikacademy.com

Sigils for this book are housed at

https://davepsychic.com/goddesses-of-hm-sigils/

Magick Books by David Thompson

Available as EPUB, Paperback and Hardcover (*)

High Magick Series

- High Magick 101
- Daemons of High Magick
- Daemons and the Law of Attraction*
- Magick of Astaroth*
- Daemons of Fortune*
- Lilith, Goddess of Darkness and Light*
- Asmodeus King of Daemons*

Grecian Magick Series

- Magick of Apollo
- Magick of Hermes
- Magick of Aphrodite
- Magick of Fortuna*
- Greco-Roman Wealth Magick*
- Magick of the Sirens/Magick of the Muses

Fiction Novels by David Thompson

The Furies Series

- Angels of Vengeance

www.ingramcontent.com/pod-product-compliance
Lightning Source LLC
LaVergne TN
LVHW010914110826
845149LV00013B/2357

* 9 7 8 1 9 6 1 7 6 5 0 0 9 *